THE
SUCCESS
PRINCIPLE

Dave Johnson

HARVEST HOUSE PUBLISHERS
Irvine, California 92714

Acknowledgment:

Except where otherwise noted, Scripture quotations are taken from The Modern Language Bible—The New Berkeley Version © 1945, 1959, 1969. Zondervan Publishing House.

THE SUCCESS PRINCIPLE

© 1976 by Harvest House Publishers, Irvine, CA 92714
Library of Congress Catalog Card Number 76-17365
ISBN 0-89081-052-4

Printed in the United States of America

To my wife,
Connie
without whom this book
would not have been possible.

CONTENTS

INTRODUCTION

Success ranks high in the priority of values for many people. There is no lack of strivers who are urgently seeking for success in their endeavors. In the face of the popularity of success, I have never heard one person exclaim: "My goal is to be a failure!" "I am really working hard to become a failure!" "It is my utmost desire to be able to say that I am the best failure the world has ever known!" Neither you nor I have ever heard anyone make those preposterous statements, because failure is not popular. No one wants to fail! But if failure is so unpopular, why is it that so many people fail? There must be a reason. The purpose of this book is to present the answer to these questions.

One of the most popular subjects found on the shelves of book stores is how to become more successful. Hundreds of authors have very helpfully presented their experiences concerning how they achieved success. Thousands of people have been inspired and uplifted by these individuals who have shared their secrets of abundant prosperity. Yet, are these ideas really secrets available to a select few? Are they merely recent discoveries which have been hidden by the darkness of time? Or are these principles of success which have been available to all of us throughout the generations, but we simply have not recognized them for what they are and the inherent power contained in their application?

In what form have these ideas been available to us for so long? For thousands of years these ideas have been accessible to us in the homes of many people in the form of their family Bible. In the pages of the Bible we have had each one of the principles of success explained many times so that we could have long ago benefited from their suggestions.

It is the old story of application though. You can lead a horse to water but you can't make him drink. BUT, you can feed him salt and he will want desperately to drink. Not everyone will heed the principles of success contained in the pages of the Bible or in the stories of other success books, but those who do absorb and express these principles in their everyday living, will benefit from them and live a more abundant life.

Why another book on the subject of success when there are so many other excellent ones already available? For one major reason! To place in perspective an important fact concerning the claimed original authorship of each of these success concepts! Even though some of these ideas may have appeared in print over one hundred years ago, they are still very late in coming when you consider the original recording of these ideas. In the pages of this book you will discover that each of these important success concepts were FIRST introduced in the Bible. For 2000 years, these ideas have been at our fingertips. This book intends to relate these ideas to the recent success authors and show how their ideas are sound in principle because they were endorsed many years ago by the inspired writers of the Bible. In the words of Solomon, "there is nothing new under the sun!" (Ecclesiastes 1:9).

There is one other major difference in the presentation of the success ideas in the Bible and those of the recent authors. These recent success writers vividly explain how they experienced desperate times to elicit the urgent principles of success they claim will work for you as well, but they lack one vital ingredient to the total culmination of lasting happiness and abundant success. That important missing ingredient is that though they explain HOW to achieve success, they do not give you the strength with which to accomplish this goal. They tell you what it is that must be done in order to experience prosperity, but do not provide the strength and energy through which to attain this sought after level of living. The Bible, however, not only lists the necessary ingredients prerequisite for success, but explains that the author of the book will provide you with unlimited strength with which to achieve "IMMEASURABLY FAR BEYOND WHATEVER YOU ASK OR THINK!" (Ephesians 3:20).

As you fill in your own definition of success throughout this book may you discover true happiness and success in the accomplishing and enjoyment of a higher and more abundant life!

David W. Johnson

1

CREATING THE
CONDITIONS FOR SUCCESS

When we place a seed into the ground and expect it to grow and produce after its kind, we have to insure the proper conditions for growth. A seed planted in dry ground will remain static because there is no moisture to soften the outer hard shell allowing the inner seed to react with its environment.

Certain mineral nutrients are needed in the ground to feed and encourage the growth of the tiny seed. As we insure these proper growing conditions we know that we will eventually be able to enjoy the produce of this seed.

Our subconscious mind is like the fertile ground in that certain conditions are necessary to obtain the produce of success. The seeds of success which we place in our subconscious are in the form of thoughts. Everything around us was originally a thought in the mind of some person—right from the beginning when God conceived of the world in His mind. As this thought seed is cultivated in a proper environment it germinates and grows into the real form of the original thought. We then can enjoy the produce of that thought.

Along the way, weeds may choke and obstruct the development of the seed we place in the ground, or because of lack of moisture and sun it may never develop into its full God given potential. Great care must be given to this tiny seed to insure its full development.

Corinne, my mother-in-law, is the only person I know who can seemingly violate this rule. It seems that the only thing she has to do is to walk among her flowers and they grow. She just has the knack to make things grow. Her garden is beautiful! Once I got the urge to plant some vegetables. I took care to prepare the ground and properly plant the seeds. Everything was okay until I forgot to water them for several days and then it was too late. That ended the vegetables and my career in gardening! It is absolutely essential that proper attention be given to a tiny seed when placed into the ground.

Thought seeds require even more care. If weeds (in the form of negative thoughts) choke its growth by saying "I don't believe it can be done," or "It's impossible," or "You can't," or "Don't try," or "Why waste the energy and time," it will die before it reaches maturity. If we never expose that thought seed to the sunshine and warmth of faith in the idea, it will die a premature death. If the soil of our mind does not contain the correct nutrients to encourage successful growth, it will never reach its full growth.

The correct condition to contribute to success ideas according to *Think and Grow Rich,* by Napoleon Hill, is that we encourage positive emotions and discourage the presence of negative emotions. Hill explains that the negative emotions are fear, jealousy, hatred, revenge, greed, superstition and anger. The positive emotions are desire, faith, love, sex, enthusiasm, romance, and hope. He explains that the subconscious mind is a delicate force and will respond only in the direction of those thoughts which are fed into it. When we feed negative thoughts into it, it will return after their kind to us. A positive thought cannot live in the presence of negative ideas. Only as we encourage positive emotions (faith, hope and love) can we expect the positive produce in the form of success.

When I first read these words of Napoleon Hill it became immediately apparent to me that I had read them somewhere else. Paul the Apostle had said practically the same thing two thousand years before when he affirmed the importance of "accentuating the positive and eliminating the negative" in Galatians 5:19-23.

> "Now the works of the flesh are in evidence, such as adultery, unchastity, impurity, lewdness, idolatry, magic, animosities, hatred, jealousy, bad temper, dissensions, a factional spirit, heresies, envy, drunkenness, carousings and everything of the kind. But the Spirit's fruition is love, joy, peace, an even temper, kindness, goodness, fidelity, gentleness, self-control."

Paul is guiding us along the same paths in terms of thoughts which will cause our subconscious storehouse of ideas to return to us the success in every endeavor we wish. In I Corinthians 13:13 he states: there remain, then, FAITH, HOPE, LOVE, these three; but the greatest of these is love.

Harold Sherman said in *Your Key to Happiness,* "Fear knocked at the door, faith answered and no one was there!" A dynamic statement, indeed!

Perfect love casts out fear. A subconscious mind which is fed the positive thoughts of faith, hope and love is bound to be successful. The absence of fear is faith in the inner power of God to guide us into higher levels of success. The Proverb tells us "above all that you guard, watch over your heart [subconscious mind] because out of it are the sources of life." Dwelling on negative emotions will produce negative sources and negative results, but faith in the principles of God will eliminate the negativism of fear and produce positive sources of prosperity! It is a principle of God!

The famous psychiatrist Dr. Paul Tournier explains that "every act of physical, psychological or moral disobedience of God's purpose is an act of wrong living and has its inevitable consequences." He explains that the effect of "hate, evil, gloom, and depression can be devastating upon mankind!"

When in New York City once, I had the opportunity of attending the Marble Collegiate Church where Dr. Norman Vincent Peale is the minister. I had always wanted to hear him speak in person and my anticipation was not unrewarded. He spoke on the subject "The Motivation that Really Motivates!" In his message he used this story to illustrate the very point that we have been discussing in this chapter. He was on his way to speak to a group of businessmen in Chicago. As he was riding in the back seat of the taxicab, Chicago was experiencing one of its many storms. He was already too close for comfort in reaching his destination on time when a stoplight delayed him even more. He explained that he soon found out why that stoplight had caused him to stop. As he was waiting for the light to turn to green, he noticed a gas station on the opposite corner which had a huge banner flopping in the heavy wind. It was difficult to read the message of the banner because it was so active, but as he finally got the complete phrase, he explained that he also got another sermon topic as well. The message: "A CLEAN ENGINE PRODUCES POWER!"

2

THE SUCCESS OF BELIEVING

Claude M. Bristol has authored an inspiring book entitled *The Magic of Believing*. In this book he explains
that there is one common strand woven throughout the
many cultures and religions he has investigated. This
common strand evidences itself in the fact that the
people of these cultures have as a part of their philosophy, whether primitive or civilized, that if they believe
that something will take place it will happen. In the
primitive cultures embracing the belief in the witch
doctor, they ascribe to him the powers to cause something to happen if he just speaks the word. Our modern
interpretations of primitive witchcraft would understand that what he says usually happens not because of
his special powers, but because those people involved
believe so intensely that they will be affected by his
words that it usually takes place. It is the power of
believing that causes these things to happen, Bristol
explains.

Modern philosophy asserts that if you have confidence in your abilities (literally believing in yourself)
you can accomplish those things that you may have
originally considered impossible. Dr. Norman Vincent

Peale begins his highly popular book *The Power of Positive Thinking* with this vital statement: "Believe in yourself! Have faith in your abilities! Without a humble but reasonable confidence in your own powers you cannot be successful or happy. But with sound self-confidence you can succeed." The Bible speaks about a power which God has given us through the ability to believe. We as humans are the only creatures with this supernatural ability. All other animals respond only to instinct, or if there is any degree of understanding beyond instinct in these animals, it is a very low level intelligence that does not include the ability to imagine a higher state of living than that into which they are locked.

The supernatural part of this principle of success is found in the human ability to believe. This power can work against as well as for us. It can defeat us if we believe that we cannot achieve beyond what we have already accomplished. We're limited because of supernatural negative forces which inject inhibiting, debilitating influences into our thinking. However, the power of believing is still working because we are believing negative thoughts about our abilities. If we believe the positive—that there is no limit to the extent to which we can achieve—then this power will work constructively for us towards a great degree of success because we engage the supernatural powers of God to speed and direct us towards our plans.

Dr. David Schwartz affirms this fact in his book *The Magic of Thinking Big*. He says: "when you believe something is impossible, your mind goes to work for you to prove why. But, when you believe, really believe, something can be done, your mind goes to work for you and helps you to find the ways to do it."

Mark 9:23 explains that the power of believing is

responsible for differing levels of accomplishment. Mark tells us: "everything is possible for a believer!" Do you wonder why some people are able to achieve more than others? It is because they *believe* that they can achieve to a greater extent. You have heard of the man who did the impossible before somebody told him that it had already been tried and found to be impossible! Do you remember the old cliche: "you can no more do that than fly to the moon"!

Jesus told the blind man who begged Him to restore his sight: "your faith has restored your sight." He also told the woman who begged that the demon be cast out of her daughter: "O woman, your faith is great; be it as you desire." In these and many other miracles the key was the faith that they had in Jesus' power. Faith in someone is the same as believing in that person. "If you have faith the size of a mustard seed, you will be able to move this mountain from here to there." Of course, we may not want to move any mountains around, but we may want to overcome some problems which seem like mountains to us. Believing that we can will generate the power to accomplish what we desire, according to the Word of God.

Dr. Wernher von Braun, the father of modern space flight says: "there would not be a single great accomplishment in the history of mankind without faith ... Any man who strives to accomplish something needs a degree of faith in himself. And when he takes on a challenge that requires more moral strength than he can muster, he needs faith in God."

3

COMPUTERIZED SUCCESS

One of the most interesting discoveries in the last one hundred years is that we have a two part mind. Thomas Jay Hudson, in *The Law of Psychic Phenomenon*, explained that we have an objective and a subjective mind. The objective mind controls decision making in the day-to-day process. It is the faculty through which we are aware of our environment. For instance, if we are hungry, the objective mind (sometimes referred to as the conscious mind) decides what and how much we will eat.

The subjective mind (or subconscious) operates below the level of awareness. It controls all of the involuntary bodily acts such as breathing, bodily repair, coordination of motor muscles, and a host of other vital functions necessary to sustain life.

The two part mind was mentioned in the Bible thousands of years ago in Proverbs 3:5. "Trust in the Lord with all your heart [heart is the subjective or subconscious mind] and lean not on your own understanding [objective or conscious mind]." The Bible stresses the urgency of trusting in the Lord when it says "He who trusts in his own heart is a fool" (Proverbs 28:26). We only connect with this inner power when we trust in the Lord completely.

Maxwell Maltz speaks of this two part mind in a different way. In his book *Psycho-Cybernetics* this highly successful plastic surgeon explains that we have a mind and a computer. He explains that the science of cybernetics (the study of how computers operate) can be applied to the way our subconscious mind operates. The way we program our subconscious mind for specific determined results is so exact that it resembles the way in which a computer must be programmed with information.

If a computer is programmed with nonsensical information it will return an answer which is jumbled; however, if it is fed sensible input it will return a logical answer. This fact is stated in computer language: Good In, Good Out; Garbage In, Garbage Out, or G-I-G-O for short.

Computers figure payroll for large masses of employees, determine interest at any given time for deposits of thousands of people, chart courses for space craft to distant destinations, run unattended trains, allow aircraft to fly themselves, and hundreds of other functions which would require many man hours to duplicate. It is said that one computer can do in three minutes a mathematical equation that would take one man with pencil and paper 37 years to do!

Even as amazing as electronic computers are, the computer of the mind is even more astounding. The subconscious has an incredible memory because it never forgets! You may wonder why it is that you forget things so often. You actually don't forget, it is just that you haven't learned how to obtain stored information from your mind's memory banks. Those who demonstrate fantastic memories haven't created these powers, they have just learned to "release" inherent natural powers of memory. When the Bible speaks of this inner power (Eph. 3:20) it is referring to the God-given power contained in our subconscious computer mind. Electronic computers occupy many square feet, whereas the computer of the mind is only three pounds of mass! When you realize that this tiny lump of protoplasm can hold infinitely more information than the electronic giants you begin to understand why Paul said "we are fearfully and wonderfully made!"

Computers are a recent technological development and have advanced civilization to an astounding level of progress. Dr. Maltz has presented us with a significant understanding of the human mind when he explains that we can program the mind for specific success if we feed it with success ideas just as we can expect failure if we bombard it with information garnered from the trash peddlers. This is employing the G-I-G-O principle with respect to our subconscious mind.

Just think—one hundred years ago nobody had ever heard of the G-I-G-O principle as applied to computers, because there were no computers as yet. No one had ever thought of applying the G-I-G-O formula to the human mind in those days because no one had been exposed to this principle—or had they?

Could it be possible that for thousands of years the G-I-G-O principle has been available and that we have not understood how to avail ourselves of its benefits? Do you suppose that it is possible that the Bible is such a forerunner of success principles that the G-I-G-O principle is found within its pages? Read Matthew 12:35 and come to your own conclusions:

"A good man brings out good things from good accumulations, and a bad man brings out bad things from bad accumulations.

Is that not the G-I-G-O principle given to us thousands of years ago in the inspired Word of God? Good In, Good Out; Bad In, Bad Out!

We can literally program ourselves for whatever results we want in terms of success or failure by taking care of what we feed into our mind computer. Jeremiah 17:10 records: "I the Lord search the heart and test the inner self to give to everyone according to his ways, in accordance with the fruit of his actions."

4

"I CAN"
The Confidence of Success

Almost every book dealing with how to become more successful includes a discussion on how to have confidence in yourself. They explain that a belief in yourself is of utmost importance in being successful and that without this high self esteem it is most difficult to attain a high degree of achievement.

Miss Shirley Cothran who was Miss America for 1975 explained in a nationally televised interview that when she first entered the local Corpus Christi, Texas beauty pageant she did so with some doubt in her ability to win. In fact, she admitted, she didn't think she would win! The result: she lost!

A year later, after she realized that she could do all things through Christ, she entered again the local pageant with the powerful "I CAN" attitude motivating her. She won not only the local and state pageants, but the cherished Miss America Beauty Pageant!

Confidence in yourself is believing that you can accomplish above average tasks; that you can achieve beyond the normal level of performance. It is believing that your talents are those which will lead you to be able to do almost anything to which you set your mind. It is respecting yourself; having faith in your abilities, in essence, loving yourself.

The Bible speaks of the necessity of self esteem in the second commandment: "Love your neighbor as yourself." It is important that we love our neighbor, but the first and last words of this commandment indicate a vital key to success: "Love yourself." If you follow the intent of this commandment, you will do the things which will allow you to be able to perform above average providing an added measure of confidence in yourself. Loving yourself is respecting yourself and having confidence in yourself. It all fits together as one important success principle.

A book written by Ben Sweetland is entitled *I CAN* and creates the urgency of inspiration within our soul to believe that WE CAN achieve those lofty plans we secretly desire. Mr. Sweetland is a master in presenting us with motivating principles which lead us on to greater confidence in the fact that WE CAN by believing that WE CAN! It is a principle which has been a part of the inspired Word of God and which Paul the Apostle wrote about many years before. Paul spoke of this confidence to achieve when he said: "I CAN do all things through Christ!" Notice that there is no qualification in Paul's statement. He didn't say: "I CAN do lots of things through Christ; or I CAN do more things than I ever thought I could," but he expressed complete confidence in the strength provided by Christ to achieve: "I CAN do ALL THINGS through Christ which strengthens me!" What confidence is exhibited in that dynamic statement!

The Winner's Edge

Don Sutton of the Los Angeles Dodgers once re-marked that "all you need to be successful is to be a little bit better than the next person. This gives you the edge on your competition!" He went on to explain that "Jesus Christ gives me the winner's edge." He had learned that "with God, nothing is ever impossible."

This totality of achievement is recorded in I John 3:21-22:

> "Loved ones, in case our hearts do not con-
> demn us, then we draw near to God with
> CONFIDENCE and whatever we may ask
> we receive from Him, for we observe His
> injunctions and practice what is pleasing in
> His sight."

These verses explain that we can draw near to God WITH CONFIDENCE, if we observe His injunctions. The injunctions referred to, of course, include those success principles which are woven throughout its pages.

Confidence is a "trust in or reliance upon something or someone; a belief in a person or thing," according to the dictionary. When we trust God for this confident attitude we are not relying on our "own understand-ing" but are basing our expectant confident attitude upon solid principles of success. Then our self-confidence is not overbearing nor unappealing to others because the "self" in our "self-confidence" is not "our-self" but none other than God "Him-self." Then, as it says in Proverbs 3:23, "You will walk your way confidently, and will not stumble."

5

YOU ARE WHAT YOU THINK

Most philosophers support one fundamental concept whether they are of the Western or Eastern world, of the ancient or present age. That concept is that

"You become what you think about."

William James said in the early 1900's that one of the most important discoveries of his time was not the electric light or the automobile, but that "man can change his attitude by changing what he thinks about." Others say that "you are what you hold in the focus of your imagination," or that "you are the sum total of all your thoughts up to the present moment." Emerson stated that "As fast as you conform your life to the pure idea in your mind, that will unfold its great proportions."

It's unfortunate that each of these philosophers had to "discover" this concept individually since the Bible proclaimed this very fact over 2000 years ago in Proverbs 23:7.

"As a man thinks in his heart [mind] so is he."

In Galatians 6:7 it records:

> "Whatever a man sows [in terms of thoughts] that shall he also reap."

Each of these statements indicate that we "become what we think about." The thoughts which we hold in the center of our imagination are the future manifestations of reality in our life. If you reflect for a moment upon those ideas which you allow to hold a greater proportion of time in your mind, perhaps you will recognize that this is what you really represent. One man said it this way: "watch what a man pays ATTENTION to, and I'll tell you what his subconscious INTENTIONS are."

What are you paying attention to? What are the things which claim the forefront of your imagination? These thoughts, ideas and concepts mirror the real you. By devoting so much time to these thoughts, they become the things in which you are placing your faith! Since you think so much about these thoughts and they occupy such a great amount of your time, these are the real things in which you believe and put your trust. In reality, they are the thoughts with which you feel most comfortable. They represent what you are becoming: the moral and spiritual code to which you will subscribe tomorrow. Dr. David Schwartz said in his book *The Magic of Thinking Big* "You are what you think you are." Your future success or failure will reflect the essence of your present deepest thoughts. Conversely, you are today the sum total of those thoughts which have previously occupied stage center in your awareness. If you consider yourself to be a success you are so because you have embraced successful concepts. If you think on dynamic, uplifting thoughts, then this represents your present character.

Jay has always been the kind of person who is conservative and cautious in whatever he does. He has held the same job for twenty five years and in the same position. He has not advanced in his responsibilities because he has always avoided any opportunity which would require him to make a change in his thinking.

Though he has voiced the desire to get "into something else" he held fast to his conservative cautious thinking, and avoided "taking any chances."

By feeding yourself limiting and self-debilitating thoughts, you become the kind of individual who reflects an "I can't" or "it's impossible" type of attitude. However, if you believe that through Christ you can do all things you will become one who can accomplish almost anything to which you put your mind.

The more we engage in the process of directing our mental input the more control we'll acquire and the easier it will be for us to direct our habits which will lead us to a greater degree of success and accomplishment. The result will be that we will become more dynamic, more motivated and develop a greater ability to work with others.

6

THE EXPECTANCY OF SUCCESS

As we program our mind with the success principles in the Bible we begin to develop the faith necessary to move the mountainous problems in our life. As this faith continues to grow, it brings with it an attitude of "expectancy." This attitude of expectancy is very important to the appropriation of this inner power for the solution to problems and the answers to the desires of our heart. It helps us to develop the faith to believe that we have already received our requests and overcome our negative hindrances. Without this attitude of expectancy, the attainment of a greater degree of success becomes a very difficult task. It becomes work, particularly in the field of selling. It is so much a part of a salesman's tools in the presentation of his product to a prospect that if he doesn't BELIEVE in his abilities to present the product and to influence the customer to purchase, it becomes a very difficult job for him to sell. He has to "EXPECT" to make a sale.

In his book, *Secrets of Closing Sales,* Charles Roth suggests that one way to close more sales is to employ what is termed as the "assumptive" close. This is to maintain an assumptive attitude towards the fact that the customer will buy. He has to continually assume that the customer will purchase the product during his entire presentation. It is necessary to assume that they haven't come into the store just for their health but instead to purchase the product. This is the expectant attitude. If the salesman presents his product in such a way that demonstrates the confidence that he expects them to purchase, chances are much greater that he will sell, rather than merely obtain the response "we'll think it over"!

A truly expectant attitude reflects itself in the fact that a salesman believes that he will sell his product. He believes that he will make a sale as a result of what he does and the fact that he expects them to buy. The expectant attitude and the fact of believing that he will attain that for which he is working go hand in hand.

Dan worked for me as a salesman for several years. Everybody liked him immediately. He had been a carpenter just several years before and had not been in sales until recently. But Dan could really sell! When asked what the secret of his success was, he merely replied: "I just try to help them get what they want!" I am not sure that he even knew what it was that caused him to be so successful, but as I tried to analyze his sales techniques, I am sure of one thing. He *expected* the people to purchase as a result of his helpfulness. Everything he said was directed towards the end that they would take the product home with them. Never once did his attitude infer that he thought they wouldn't buy. He just assumed that this was the reason they came into his store in the first place. Dan reports that many of his customers tell him that they didn't come in expecting to purchase anything, but yet they ended up buying! As a result of his expectant attitude, Dan was a top-notch salesman.

To continue the use of the sales illustration a bit further, an expectant attitude will not be the result of a flimsy sales presentation nor of an unprepared demonstration. The expectant attitude is the result of an individual who has self-confidence in himself that he can influence and motivate people to take action immediately. One gets this expectant attitude only as a result of preparing himself and perfecting his abilities to sell and by the "hearing" of ideas relating to selling! As a result of a strong expectant attitude he then develops the ability to believe that he has already received the sale or whatever it is that he desires.

The need for preparation in any field is obvious. If we have no solid foundation upon which to base our belief that we will receive that for which we pray, then our lack of self-confidence will be quite apparent. Doubt rather than expectant faith will be the order of the day. Dr. David Schwartz says in his book *The Magic of Thinking Big*, "to accomplish something, we must PLAN to accomplish something." It could also be said in this way, "to accomplish something we must EXPECT to accomplish something!"

Just as a professional salesman prepares himself to make a sale through obtaining product knowledge he then follows through by expecting to make a sale. In preparing for success it is essential that we prepare ourselves for prosperity by obtaining "product knowledge" through programming ourselves with success principles. The mind is the only organ in the human body which once stretched to the dimensions of a new idea never returns to its original size. By expanding our expectancy of success to new proportions we will discover that we have a promise made by God concerning success in Joshua 1:8-9:

"Constantly remind the people about these laws, and you yourself must think about them every day and every night so that you will be sure to obey all of them. For only then will you succeed. Yes, be bold and strong! Banish fear and doubt! For remember, the Lord your God is with you wherever you go."

An additional promise emphasizes this success expectancy even more intensely since He promised that "His word will not return to us void but will accomplish the task for which it was intended!"

Success is yours if you expect to receive it! This is the message of Mark 11:24. "Whatever you ask in prayer, believe that you received it and it shall be yours." BELIEVE that you RECEIVED! Received is in the past tense indicating that your belief should be so strong that it is like you already have "received" that for which you ask! That is powerful belief! That is also a powerful attitude of expectancy!

7

THE AFFIRMATION OF SUCCESS

We are in a constant process of change, both mentally and physically. Every part of our body is constantly being rebuilt through cellular replacement. The Bible points out that we need to "daily renew our mental attitude." Someone once said "anything that is alive is growing." A stagnant pool of water breeds disease and begins to smell!

Our bodies change daily for better or worse. If we live active, energetic lives, our bodies constantly renew themselves. If we become slothful in our exercise program, we deteriorate!

Our attitudes reflect the condition of our mental state. A healthy, dynamic attitude reflects a mind which considers vital thoughts and ideas. A negative attitude indicates mental sluggishness and limiting thoughts.

My wife, Connie, told me that she experienced a dramatic change in attitude when we moved to Chicago several years ago. Before this time we lived in Tucson for several years, and Connie became involved in selling real estate and motor homes. For a gal who had never sold anything before, she did extremely well! In the real estate field, she completely sold out one sub-division practically by herself! Of course, my buttons were poppin' because I was married to such a smart young lady!

It was easier for her to become involved with activities in Tucson than in Chicago because she heard so many stories about the strange things that happen in the huge city by Lake Michigan! After we moved to Chicago, Connie was unable to use her real estate license since they are not transferable from one state to another. Chicago seemed to her to be a strange, unfriendly, and dangerous world, almost like the Proverbs say: "there is a lion in the way; a lion is in the streets." She felt herself begin to withdraw from the outside world because of this unfamiliarity and to become secure in her own little home! Her attitude became slothful and sluggish, never wanting to go anywhere—not even to church!

It wasn't long before this sharp little gal suddenly took note of what was happening to her and she grabbed hold of herself. She said that she actually had to push herself out of the door—hating every step of it, but knowing that she had to do this or shrivel up to a drab existence! She knew down deep that there was more to life than what she was temporarily experiencing and so she took steps to begin to renew her mental attitude by placing into her mind new and more challenging thoughts.

She felt that because the children were now in their teens (and older) that she could take on a part time job. She did, and it wasn't long before she was asked to take more responsibility in a full time position. She is now quite happy and well adjusted in her activities. But if she hadn't taken the steps to renew her mental attitude with the infusion of new thoughts, she might have stayed home in her own private little world and become more and more bored and unhappy with herself.

We ARE the assemblage of our attitudes. Words constitute the structure of thought and form the basis of concepts, ideas and attitudes. Every word that you utter and thought that you think about determines what you are becoming daily. The Scriptures support this in Matthew 12:37:

> "By your words you will be acquitted [set free], and by your words you are condemned."

Each individual word and thought forms concepts upon which you base your personal philosophy of life and determines what you are becoming. Someone once proclaimed that "every man daily declares himself by his words and actions." Thoughts are seeds which, when planted in the fertile soil of the mind, bear the produce according to their kind.

I recall a conversation in which the owners of a company were concerned about their public image. They correctly realized that the public's conception of the company's image in the market place directly influenced the extent to which they would purchase their product. Not only was this public image determined by the quality of the product and its serviceability, but also by the individuals which represented that company in the market place.

Their conversation jumped from one phase of image building to another until it centered upon Wendell. Poor Wendell was somebody that we all just had to tolerate. He was a pretty nice guy once you got to know him, but unfortunately, most people would not give him that much time. Wendell had a trait about him which made him say things like they really were. He wouldn't exercise any caution in how he would say something, even for the sake of public relations or someone else's feelings. Everybody in the office understood this trait, but those in the market place were usually not ready for his abrasiveness, and as a result it cost us some important business occasionally. Some of the executives claimed that he was just a "peasant at heart" and wasn't interested in the social amenities required in business. Wendell was daily confirming this evaluation of himself by his words and actions!

When God formed the heavens and the earth and placed man and the animals on the earth he added a phrase to His initial founding words to direct the ongoing process of reproduction of both animal and plant life. He said in Genesis 1:24,

"Let the earth bring forth living creatures
AFTER THEIR KIND, livestock, reptiles
and wild beasts AFTER THEIR KIND."

The phrase which maintains order in the reproduction of the species is that they reproduce "AFTER THEIR KIND." This is not only true in the animals and plant life, but especially so in our thought life. Every thought and word is reproduced "AFTER THEIR KIND." When you grumble about circumstances by complaining: "I just don't seem to understand it," you are condemning your mind to the fate of having to interpret conditions through a dense fog. The more you react in this manner to conditions by complaining: "I don't understand it," the more difficult it will become for you to understand, and the more things will happen TO you rather than FOR you! Every word and thought is reproduced "AFTER THEIR KIND." It is my impression that there are two classes of people in this world! The first are those who MAKE things happen, and the second are those TO WHOM things happen. Your words determine the category to which you belong!

Sometimes these convicting statements seem to slip out of our mouth without much thought; however, the effect that they command can be devastating! I recently heard one of my acquaintances declare: "I'm older now, and my 'head' is getting slower in understanding things." What a severe sentence he is inflicting upon himself! It's true though. After he alerted me to this desperate fact, he did seem to be aging faster than ever before and was slower to comprehend various ideas presented to him—a fact I would not have noticed had he not pointed it out to me!

Proverbs 17:28 declares:

> "Even a fool when he is silent is thought to be wise, and he who keeps his lips closed is considered intelligent."

By consistently recounting to yourself: "I never seem to get ahead," you force yourself to live at a subservient level in which you'll find more than your share of people telling you what to do! When you complain: "I never get any breaks," you'll condemn yourself to an uneventful life; a future which seems to avoid exhibiting any fortunate breaks. If you whine that life is just a drag, you're dooming yourself to a drab and tedious life. If you preface things about which you talk with "I can't," you'll find that life will be difficult. By preceding the description of your responsibilities with the epitaph: "I don't like my work," you'll find that your job will be dull and unchallenging. When you proclaim that many tasks are difficult for you to do, that's precisely the destiny with which you'll be saddled. You'll learn that many of your tasks are beyond your power and discouragingly incomprehensible. By reacting to various challenges with: "that's impossible to do," then this is specifically the way they will present themselves: they will be impossible for you to complete, because everything is reproduced "AFTER THEIR KIND."

Norman Vincent Peale wrote in his book *Enthusiasm Makes the Difference,* "You can change your thinking and thereby change your life by deliberately imaging into your subconscious good ideas [words], positive images, instead of negative ones. You are constantly in a state of becoming. And you *do* become what you think!"

The book entitled *The New TNT–Miraculous Power Within You* written by Harold Sherman suggests that "there is tremendous power in spoken and written words, when they are really meant and have strong feelings behind them." Perhaps this is what was meant in Job 22:28. "Thou shalt also decree a thing, and it shall be established unto thee."

How to Liberate Yourself from Impossible Thinking

If you find yourself snagged with negative restrictions prefacing your thoughts and ideas and discover that your words are imprisoning you, there is a method that can reverse these effects and release you from the problems that have been acquired from impossible thinking. Instituting this positive action may be accomplished through the power of positive affirmations. Many of the verses in the Bible are positive declarations of faith which inspire us to dynamic attitudes of success and thinking which leads to prosperous living. Through this practice we are promised success and prosperity in Joshua 1:8-9. If you ponder these success concepts on a daily basis, they will then reproduce "AFTER THEIR KIND."

Personal Affirmations

These affirmations may be of our own personal design. Perhaps you know of people who are prone to catch every sickness that comes along. They are always pointing out some ache or pain that forms their most vital point of conversation. Indeed, two minutes of verbal interchange will bring you up to date on all of their visits to doctors, dentists, or psychiatrists, and will tell you of all the remedial prescriptions they have to take to combat their many illnesses and all of the germs which are chasing them! Their conversation includes these negative affirmations: "I just never seem to feel very good, I always have a headache!" "If there is something going around, I always seem to catch it!"

Mary Jane had never known a day in her life during which she wasn't suffering from some ailment. She always managed to recover from one of her problems just in time to get involved with another one. She was either in the hospital for various tests to discover some illusive illness, or claimed that the doctor had ordered complete bed rest because of physical exhaustion.

Her conversation included a myriad of negative affirmations describing her unfortunate physical problems. If it wasn't a recent operation she had to endure, it was some unusual medication that was necessary to correct some imbalance in her system. Of course, she included an array of allergies to which there seemed to be no solution, and other problems for which medical science has not yet discovered a cure.

Have you heard overweight people tell you that everything they eat turns to fat while the nice and trim ones proudly exclaim that they can eat everything and anything and never gain any weight? While these statements are their own personal affirmations and produce like results in their lives, the fat statements don't bother me too much, but the skinny ones really get to me. The Bible says that we are not to envy others, but I sure would like to look like some of the skinny ones I have seen—probably because I am still working on about 15 to 20 extra pounds of dessert I carry with me.

Research has revealed that there are people who are psychosomatically "well" to the same extent that others talk themselves into believing that they are "sick" to accommodate their life style. These "sick" people are trapped in a mental rut which differs from a grave only in that the ends have not yet been defined! They are being condemned by their words because whatever they are decreeing unto themselves is being established! Dr. Paul Tournier states in his book *The Healing of Persons* that wrong thinking can have physically devastating effects. He continues by saying that "most illnesses do not come like a bolt out of the blue. The ground is prepared for years through many causes, including improper thinking!"

If your conversation is punctuated with some of these negative, inflictive words, you can reverse the nauseous effects of these accusatory statements by saying: "I feel marvelous: I feel wonderful all of the time." These are simple, yet powerful, personal, positive affirmations.

You may object by protesting: "what good is it to say that I feel good when I really don't feel good most of the time?" That's not the point! The Bible implies that you feel badly because you have psychosomatically condemned yourself through your negative statements about how badly you feel! We are urged by the Scriptures to maintain a positive attitude at all times! "In everything give thanks!" "This is the day which the Lord has made, let us be glad and rejoice in it!" "Rejoice in every good thing!" "Rejoice, and again I say rejoice!" You are the result of what you've been telling yourself because everything reproduces AFTER THEIR KIND! "By your words you will be acquitted (set free), and by your words you are condemned."

If you start to sing a new song which is orchestrated with positive harmony, eventually you will assume whatever characteristics are suggested by your new, vibrant melody! So by proclaiming: "I feel wonderful, I feel great," your health will eventually assume melodic proportions rather than discordant depressions. Your mind will respond in the direction of your new thoughts and to the attitude of your dynamic melody. David said: "He has put a new song in my heart! A Praise to our God!"

If you continually reaffirm: "I am becoming more and more successful," these things will eventually show themselves in your life. Your job will begin to go better, you'll interpret situations to your advantage and success rather than in terms of misery and failure. You'll be able to respond to challenges in a more positive, constructive and dynamic manner by repetitively affirming to yourself that "I am becoming more and more successful."

Here are some examples of positive affirmations:

FROM THE BIBLE:

"I CAN do all things through Christ which strengthens me."

"All things work together for good to them who love Christ."

"Blessed is the man who walks not after the advice of the wicked nor stands in the path of sinners, nor sits in the seat of scoffers! but his delight is in the law of the Lord and His law he ponders day and night. He is like a tree planted by streams of water, that yields its fruit in its season, whose leaf does not wither; and everything he does shall prosper."

"Everything is possible for a believer!"

"With God, everything is possible."

"He that believes in me shall not perish but have everlasting life."

"Thou wilt keep him in perfect peace whose mind is stayed on Thee."

"Finally, whatever is true, honorable, just, pure, lovely, kindly spoken, lofty and praiseworthy—put your mind on these. And what you have learned and received and heard and seen in me, that put into practice. And the God of peace will be with you."

GENERAL AFFIRMATIONS:

"In every way I feel better and better!"

"Everything seems to work out well for me."

"I always have lots of good ideas."

"I like people and they like me."

"Every day in every way I am getting better and better."

"I believe that through Christ I have the ability to do whatever I really want to do."

"I have been receiving some excellent increases in salary and promotions in my job."

"Don't look back unless that's the way you want to go!"

The focal power of affirmations is that you eventually believe and become what you keep telling yourself, so through the technique of positive affirmations, "Tell yourself what you want to become."

8

CHOOSING SUCCESSFUL THOUGHTS

Your future success lies in your hands! It is immediately within your reach! What happens TO or FOR you in the future is totally up to you! You possess the key which will allow you to structure the conditions of your future life—but the key is worthless unless it is used to unlock the potential of a prosperous future.

The key is dependent upon a law of God which says: "that which is sown and cultivated yields its produce!" There is a positive and negative side of this law. Those who have a habit of cultivating negative ideas realize a harvest of negative ideas. This limiting circumstance will hinder their potential success. If you are this kind of person you will be literally bound by the ropes of negative habits. "They are held fast by the ropes of their own sin" (Proverbs 5:22). It is both simple and difficult to extricate oneself from this inflictive philosophy because "people resist change." People would rather continue in their negative habits than change because they are familiar with their old circumstances. Even though they realize that they can never experience true success in their negative habit patterns, they resist changing to new patterns of thought. This is because of the human trait which resists the new and clings to the old. Because of the binding power of these habits it is difficult to change to a positive philosophy. At the same time it is simple to make this change because it only requires a change of thought. Start to apply your thinking to thoughts which renew your daily attitude, rather than to hold to those which limit your thought horizons. The change is really quite simple. It only takes a quick decision to think new positive thoughts. Since we reap what we sow we will reap the natural produce of the thought seeds we embrace. The change of habit will naturally follow the change of thoughts. Many people try to change a habit by changing appropriate actions without realizing that their habits follow the nature of their thoughts. This is why we are told to "bring every mental perception into captivity." Since these thoughts are going to grow in our mind it would seem right to examine each one to see if its potential is what we want to be evidenced in our future circumstances. It is both simple and difficult to free yourself from the negative influences of this law. The simplistic feature is evidenced if we change our thinking patterns to indicate the conditions of our future desired success. It takes a positive thought to set this change into motion.

The positive side of this law is the same power which binds those negative thinkers. It also provides power and thrust to a positive philosophy. The "I CAN" thinkers employ the power of Christ in their endeavors. Those who look for ways things CAN be done rather than why they are impossible engage God as their partner. The power within provides motivation to cause circumstances to inspire rather than destroy.

We are confronted with two powers in this life: The

power of God and the forces of Satan. These two opposing forces are sometimes given different labels such as: good and evil; negative and positive thinking; light and dark, etc. The basic forces, however, are either God or Satan. When we think positively or negatively, we are choosing sides and determining whether our future will be a success or failure. It is up to us to choose the future success we desire! Don Polston proclaims in his dynamic book *Living Without Losing* that "Satan can have no more power over you than the thought he can inject into your mind!"

Bertrand Russell discussed this problem in his book *The Conquest of Happiness*. He explained that he had a problem with negative thinking as a child. He said that because of much negative preaching (yes, preachers can be negative too) he seemed to have a habit of dwelling upon the negative aspects of Biblical teachings, instead of the power and freedom we are offered by God. He writes: "I had a habit of meditating on my sins, follies, and shortcomings. I seemed to myself—no doubt justly—a miserable specimen." He continues to explain that he learned to change his attitude by shifting his thought patterns to the positive side of the Biblical message. In this way he freed himself from the dungeons of negativism and broke the bonds which kept him from experiencing the freedom and power and love which are ours to enjoy and through which we can be lifted up to new heights of success and prosperity.

Dr. John A. Schindler stresses the importance of this process in his book: *How To Live 365 Days a Year*. He said "a person has to start in the present to acquire some maturity so that the future may be better than the past. The present and the future depend on learning new habits and new ways of looking at old problems." He indicates that one problem of failure is that ... "the patient has never learned how to control his present thinking to produce future enjoyment!"

This exciting concept is one which was experienced by another great individual many years before. This person is Paul the Apostle! He wrote in Colossians 3:2, "Apply your mind to things above, not to things on earth!" Here is another pair of opposite forces: things above suggest those concepts of freedom and power in Christ, and those things on earth point to the negative forces which only bind and constrict our potential soaring attitude which we may have through Christ. Paul even went further when he suggested certain thoughts which would be indicative of becoming partners with Christ in our endeavors. In Philippians 4:8 he recorded: "whatever is true, honorable, just, pure, lovely, kindly spoken, lofty and praiseworthy, PUT YOUR MIND ON THESE.... and the God of peace will be with you!"

How is this key employed? Its positive effects may be experienced by doing the same things that you did to acquire the habits you presently have! We all have habits, some of which are beneficial and others are undesirable. If you have ever watched someone trying to stop smoking, you know the power which a habit can possess. Proverbs says that we are held fast by the ROPES of our own sin (habits). Ropes are made up of tiny little fibers which are entwined and together become extremely strong. One fiber by itself is not very strong and can easily be broken; however, when they all exert their influence at one time the complete binding power is felt.

Habits are like ropes in the sense that they are formed by one small act at a time. If we think one negative thought, we have not formed a habit of negative thinking; however, as we add more strength to that habit by continually thinking negative thoughts, that habit is formed into an intertwined force which binds us with unbelievable strength. Ropes can be broken. So can habits be broken by forming stronger habit patterns to overcome the strength of the old ones. This is done by structuring a new habit of renewed positive thoughts. By considering those thoughts of a positive nature and rejecting negative ones we can begin to form a new pattern of thinking which will exhibit power and strength through having God as our partner. It takes one positive decision after another to form this new habit. We accomplish this task by rejecting those thoughts which will not contribute to our new positive attitude. In this way we may specifically determine our future success.

9

BE ANXIOUS FOR NOTHING

John was an analytical person and one whom I enjoyed having in my Sunday School Class. He contributed much to the class through his refreshing honesty. We were studying the Success Principles contained in the Bible. We had been considering the principle covered in Matthew 10:39 which says: "He that finds his life shall lose it; and he that loses his life for my sake shall find it." John suddenly exclaimed that he violently objected to a principle that suggests that you have to lose your life before you can find it! He explained that he has expended a great deal of time to develop his talents and abilities with which he planned to pursue a worthwhile career and attain a satisfactory life—one which he hoped would produce much results. The idea of losing all of this effort to somehow mysteriously rediscover it seemed to be too vague to be worth its effort of pursuit!

John had a point! The verse seems to be exactly opposite to what we as mortals can easily understand. It is important to remember that many principles are supernatural and are not easily understood at first. It is only through God's wisdom that we can comprehend the power contained in this principle. Sometimes it is necessary to consider another principle in conjunction with the first to completely gain the inherent meaning and application for our lives.

Our policy in the class was to have an open discussion so we could all respond to the ideas presented to us by the Holy Spirit and in that way get the greatest content in each of our meetings. All of us tossed various ideas around concerning this principle and then I suggested this concept. A tiny seed is dropped into the ground, covered over and completely forgotten. From this act, a huge tree may be produced and in that way enrich many people's lives through its beauty and eventual produce.

The key principle in this act is that the seed dies to itself and is buried. It is only then that the Laws of God are able to work and cause considerable growth to take place. The little seed has to lose its life before it can once again find it to even greater proportions.

But why, as human beings who have been given talents and abilities by God, should we have to die before we can evidence any value to God? It doesn't seem to be as valid a premise when it is personalized! I explained to the class that giving up or losing your life in the sense which is intended is not dying physically. It is not that we are to give up the desire to attain our goals and dreams nor any motivation to achieve, but the giving up of your own abilities to the God given power within each of us so that this Success Principle can effectively and efficiently work FOR US and WITH US!

I recall when I first started sales work, I was so concerned as to what I was going to say in the sales presentation that I literally memorized the recommended presentation word for word. Only a few sales were forthcoming because, of course, it sounded like it was memorized when I presented it!

I had ignored a principle of success presented in the Bible which promises us that we should "take no thought for what you shall say in that day because the words will be given you!" I have since found that this works in a most definite way in the art of selling. If you have obtained product knowledge and are sold on its benefits, you'll not have to concern yourself with the exact words to say during your presentation because they will come to you in an orderly and professional manner.

Perhaps you have experienced this letting go at various times when you get turned on to a conversational subject in which you are involved. As you get worked up on the subject, the words and thoughts come with no apparent effort on your part. They are being given to you from this inner power. It is unnecessary to engage in any conscious effort on your part, except to let go and let God work through this inner power!

Have you ever experienced a situation in which you tried desperately to figure out the solution to a problem, and fought with it for days only to give up in frustrated desperation? Shortly after this point the answer presents itself in beautiful clarity. The key here is that you gave up, relaxed your intense search for the answer and in your desperate frustration, became passive and "anxious for nothing."

A passive attitude will create the conditions necessary for God to work to bring about the solution. "You covet and you do not possess, because you ask amiss." When we covet, we intensely desire something and miss our target and do not receive that for which we wish.

Harold Sherman in his book *Your Key To Happiness*

explains that "relaxation is necessary before we can experience the power of God working for our desires." He is so right. We are told in the Bible that by "trusting in the Lord with all our heart [relaxing and becoming passive concerning our desires] and lean not on your own understanding [not relying on our own strength and knowledge] that He will direct our paths [toward the realization of our goal]" (Proverbs 3:5).

It is a most powerful force we employ when we give up of our own abilities and let the power within take over. Dr. Maxwell Maltz explained this principle in his book *Psycho-Cybernetics*. In a chapter entitled "Relax and let Your Success Mechanism Work for You" he wrote: "Our trouble is that we ignore the automatic creative mechanism and try to do everything and solve all our problems by conscious thought, or 'forebrain thinking.' "

Rich found this to be true when he finally gave up in utter exhaustion in his efforts to achieve success in his plans. For years he had detailed his desires, contemplated them day and night, charted his progress almost daily, and studied how he could improve his plans for his vast desires.

It was only after he "let go and let God" assist him in the achievement of his goals that he began to experience great success. Proberbs 16:3 says: "roll your work onto the Lord and your plans will be achieved." Rich gave up in his own efforts and quit leaning on his own understanding and rolled his work onto the Lord. It was then that he was amazed at how he began to experience the realization of his desires.

There are certain laws of God which will work for us only after we get out of the way and let them take over. There is a power within which will produce for us above and beyond that which we can ask or think of, and the way to utilize that power is to be anxious for nothing and become passive by trusting in the Lord with all our heart.

Compare the experience of achieving success to that of trying to go to sleep at night. The more we try to attain sleep, the more it evades us. It is only when we completely let go and let sleep come naturally that we experience the deep rest which accompanies nocturnal bliss.

When we "die to self," let go and wait patiently for the Lord to bring about our desires, we will experience the sweet savor of success.

10

INSTINCTIVE SUCCESS

Success, through faith, is our natural state! Failure is experienced only when we lean on our own limited understanding by not applying faith as a propellant to the finish line of our desires. Faith is a positive position announcing our belief in the unlimited inner power of God. Lack of faith is a self-limiting, negative affront to the laws of God and the principles of success. Lack of faith is fear in our own abilities to accomplish. Uniquely enough, we should fear our own personal abilities to achieve when we try in our own strength to do the things God wants to help us with. However, when we couple ourselves with the principles of success contained in the Bible we can do ALL THINGS through Christ which provides us with the strength. In ourself we are weak, but when God is with us we are a majority in any situation.

The Bible speaks a great deal about faith, and it comes down pretty hard on any activity that does not involve faith. Romans 14:23 records:

> "But the person who entertains doubts, and nevertheless eats, stands condemned, because he is not acting from FAITH, and

every act that does not spring from FAITH
is sin."

To paraphrase this verse: "If we approach any activity without faith, and with any degree of doubt, then we can expect only negative results because we're not acting INSTINCTIVELY from a position of faith in what we do." The opposite of faith is doubt. This verse suggests that faith should be an INSTINCTIVE reaction. When we touch a hot stove we instinctively spring back from it. We don't have to reason out that because my finger is touching something that hurts I had better take it away from the hot stove. Instinctively we spring back from it! Once when I was working in my shop I was using a soldering iron. After one of my sons who was about 7 or 8 years old decided to join me I warned him that the soldering iron was hot and to stay away from it. A phone call required me to leave the shop for a few minutes and while I was in conversation on the phone I heard a scream. It is amazing what young curiosity will do! He had learned early in life what instinctive action was as he was verifying my warning! This verse proclaims that "every act that does not spring (instinctive reaction) from faith is sin." That's serious talk. We should instinctively believe in our abilities to achieve through Christ's strength. It is wrong if we don't believe that strongly!

Napoleon Hill discusses this principle in his book *Think and Grow Rich*. He said: "Whatever the mind of man can CONCEIVE and BELIEVE it can ACHIEVE!" The Bible introduced this principle thousands of years before in the short but powerful statement: "everything is possible for a believer!"

We have strength and abilities of which we are not

even aware. When I was twelve years old an incident occurred which still astounds me. My dad was opening the garage door one Sunday morning only to discover that there was a flat on the rear tire. He then asked for my help in changing the tire. We used bumper jacks in those days and they had a reputation of not holding very well. I guess he thought he had set the hand brake, but it didn't hold and as he was putting the spare into the tire well, the car slid forward as it pinched my father's fingers between the tire and the fender!

Because I play piano and organ I am extra sensitive about my fingers. No doubt my dad also feels the same about his fingers since he also played the piano. After a loud scream I instinctively grabbed hold of the car and lifed the pressure of the body off of his fingers and thereby extricated him! Thank God, none were broken, just badly pinched!

This was an instinctive action on my part. There was no time to consider whether I could or could not lift the car. I acted in faith and then received the strength to follow through.

This is the key to instinctive faith: act first and then you will find the strength to do what you have set out to accomplish!

Negative forces urge us to consider all of the potential reasons why it can't be done, but instinctive faith says ACT and then receive guidance and strength from the Lord. The Proverbs declare: "man's mind plans his road but the Lord directs his steps!"

If we in our own understanding try to figure out how we will ever be able to do something, we will miss out on God's best for us and the development of more faith in our lives and never get anything worthwhile done. "Faith without works is dead!"

Since faith is a supernatural force and cannot be interpreted in terms of our five senses, when we try to figure out how God is going to answer our prayer, supply our needs, or do whatever we ask Him to do, we limit God to the potential of our five senses and to the horizon of what we can immediately understand through our own abilities.

Free God in what He can do for you by "trusting in the Lord with all your heart and not leaning on your own understanding."

11

SUCCESSFUL THINKING

Picture with me this situation: a man is listening to the radio while driving to work. It is early in the morning—about 7:15 and the traffic is exhibiting its usual dragging, start and stop tendencies. The man is only partly awake, still feeling the shock of having to get up and face another day of problems, confusion and harrassment.

As he listens to the news on the radio he hears the usual items being reported: crime, rape, divorce, riots, murder, airplane crashes, cheating and another policeman was shot! Wow, what stimulating material! Just think of the lift he gets from dwelling on these thoughts. He is really ready to face a full day of responsibility!

As he enters his office and encounters his secretary's good morning, he merely grunts in response. No wonder! Because of the negative input he has received from the radio, he is in no mood to respond cheerfully to her, nor to face any other problems that lie waiting on his desk. His secretary is hurt and thinks she has said something to the "old grump" and the whole encounter sets the tone of the day according to his negative attitude.

The rest of the day continues with this strained attitude and eventually ends in total disaster. As he ventures forth into the jostling traffic on the way home he once again feeds himself on the negative aspects of what's going on in the world. When he meets his wife upon arriving home, he grunts at her and the same act begins again causing impaired family relationships.

Or consider this episode: it is dinner time and you are agonizingly hungry. Your wife has spent considerable time in preparing a full course dinner for your enjoyment and you are looking forward to it with delighted and active taste buds. The food is being passed around to each member of the family. First comes the perfectly done roast beer, sizzling in its tantalizing aromas. Next comes the mashed potatoes followed by tasty brown rich flavored gravy! It is a pleasurable time of the day during which you can enjoy family fellowship as you partake of your wife's handiwork together.

But a terrible thing happens! As the roast beef comes to you, you pass it by! As the potatoes and gravy are handed to you, you pass it along to the next family member. Instead, you reach into the garbage pail and help yourself to some cold, unattractive potato peelings. Then you serve yourself a large helping of yesterday's left overs!

While the rest of the family enjoys the tasty, steaming items on the menu, you are stuffing yourself with the left overs and scraps found in the garbage pail. You ask: "why would someone do a terrible thing like that when there is so much good food available?" That's the whole point! Why should we dwell on negative food for the mind such as is supplied by the news medium when there is available to us the tasty morsels of the best of life! Why pour the garbage of daily living into your mind each morning when we can fill our hearts with inspiring and uplifting thoughts which will bring us happiness, peace and joy in every endeavor in life.

We can all experience the abundant life full of God's gifts. Norman Vincent Peale says: "The secret is to fill your mind with thoughts of faith, confidence and security." Our attitude depends upon the kind of thoughts which habitually fill our minds. This is the secret to abundant living. "Above all that you guard, watch over your heart (mind) for out of it are the sources of life."

In his book *The Power of Positive Thinking,* Dr. Peale explains that "whenever a negative thought concerning your personal powers comes to mind, deliberately voice a positive thought to cancel it out!" This is what the Bible means when it says to watch over your heart! Mark 4:24 warns us "to be careful to what you listen." Is the garbage pail our source, or do we receive our motivation from God Himself?

By thinking of those thoughts given to us in the Holy Word of God, we can claim this promise: "Thou wilt keep him in perfect peace whose mind is stayed on thee!"

12

THE SUCCESS OF HAPPY THINKING

Several years ago, there was a T.V. program which featured a young lady who was supposed to be a computer rather than a real person. She was to respond in the same manner in which a computer would to various situations.

As you know, when a computer is programmed with garbled information it responds with: "that does not compute"! It rejects that information as being unusable.

When illogical or garbled information was presented to the star of this television program she would answer: "that does not compute! I reject that thought!"

The idea of this young lady actually being a computer is not as far-fetched as it may seem. According to Dr. Maxwell Maltz we actually have a computer mind which can be programmed according to the science of cybernetics. We accept certain ideas as being so and our mind will respond with the appropriate action. If we reject various ideas they will not affect us in the way that they would have if we had embraced them as part of our philosophy of life.

The Bible confirms this in Proverbs 23:7, "As a man

thinks [or computes and accepts ideas] in his mind [mental computer] so is he!''

Dr. Norman Vincent Peale says "many of us manufacture our own unhappiness!" Now why should someone want to make themselves unhappy? Doesn't everyone want to be happy? Why then, is there so much misery? The answer to these questions is that most people dwell on unhappy thoughts because they don't reject them as soon as they enter their minds. Dr. Peale also says: "The happiness habit is developed by simply practicing happy thinking!" It is similar to the man who thinks he can and the one who thinks he can't—they are both right!

Why is it that people tend to think unhappy thoughts rather than positive ones which lead to happiness? We are given a clue to this natural tendency in Genesis 4:7 which alludes to the fact that negativism (sin) is a natural trait. Unhappy thoughts are negative thoughts and are not made of faith. However, if we act with faith in everything we do the miracle of happiness will lead us on to the abundant life.

How do we create the positivism of faith in our thinking? By programming our mental computer with those thoughts which will lead us on to higher forms of thinking. When working with an electronic computer we carefully choose the input we feed it; however, we are not this careful when feeding thoughts into our personal computers. Random thoughts which sneak into the mind are not passed through thought filters to "eliminate the negative" but are allowed to have their disruptive influence upon the potential peaceful state which may be ours.

In his book entitled *Your Greatest Power,* Martin Kohe explains that we can choose that which we want to become a part of our life. Our greatest power is that of CHOICE. Why then, do we choose unhappiness? It is because we think unhappy thoughts. Why do many experience failure? It is because they choose to think failure thoughts! This concept can fit any form of displeasure which you are experiencing. If you are dissatisfied with any part of your life, it is because you have been dwelling upon incorrect thoughts. You no longer have to experience this unhappiness since you can reject the thoughts which produce unsatisfactory conditions and accept only those things you want to be manifested in your life. It is your choice!

But how do you accomplish this neat trick? By following a principle set forth in the Bible. When Jesus was tempted by Satan, He employed the power of choice in His reply: "Get thee behind me Satan!" In this statement He rejected Satan's ideas and disallowed his power to compute in His mind. Modern terminology might have rephrased Jesus' reply: "That thought does not compute! I reject that idea!" Jesus literally cast that thought out of His mind and its potential power to affect Him adversely. We have this same power! We can cast out any negative thought and its destructive power by simply saying: "I reject that thought! It doesn't compute in my mind. It has absolutely no effect upon me!" Instead, the thoughts upon which I wish to dwell are: "I am happy; I am successful; I am ... (then fill in those ideas which you wish to accept and become a part of your life)!"

The E.R.A. of Success

I have used this technique for years and found it to work to successful results. One important factor concerning the successful use of this tool is that you have to *Exercise* your power of choice, *Reject* negative thoughts and *Accept* the positive thoughts to get your happiness and success cycle going for you!

Once you have developed the habit of rejecting negative thoughts and accepting the positive principles in the Bible, you will discover that by meditating on the positive principles that in everything you do you will prosper and find success—according to the Word of God!

13

THE POSSIBILITIES OF SUCCESS

How many times have you heard someone remark when confronted with a task which seemed to be beyond their ability: "That's impossible! Nobody has ever been able to do that—it can't be done!" Yet, eventually, someone did achieve that seemingly impossible task.

Quite a few years ago there was a comic strip about space travel entitled "Buck Rodgers." In that story, Buck Rodgers conquered the realms of space and sped his readers through uncharted regions of his imagination in the openness of this impossible frontier. Yet, the children of today are relatively unimpressed with the fact that man has now walked on the moon. Innumerable problems, which were at first impossible to solve, had to be isolated and identified in such a way that man could gain new perspectives from which to attack them in order to overcome the impossibilities which blocked their solution.

Almost any significant invention appeared at first to be impossible to accomplish. Think of man flying through the air like the birds—impossible because man does not have wings! Yet, today there are planes which will speed us at the rate of 1500 miles per hour. My son Stanford and I had the opportunity to visit Cape Kennedy and watch a Delta rocket being launched. As the countdown was terminated, the sudden burst of fire at the base of the rocket, the almost imperceptible upward movement of the rocket as it left the moorings of its launching pad, and then as it reached for the sky and then outer space, it seemed to be something that could only happen in a science fiction novel! As Stan read about its flight path while we were inching our way out of the parking lot he pointed out that one-half hour later as we finally extricated ourselves from the press of the parking lot congestion, the rocket was now over the equator—almost one-half of the way around the world! When the automobile was first introduced and sped us along the roads at the phenomenal rate of fifteen miles per hour, some men claimed that that speed was too much for the human body to adjust to and that speed would take our breath away! Yet someone came along and proved that the impossible was possible and then went ahead to speed us on to a better way of life!

It is a fact that as long as we consider a task to be impossible that our mind will go to great lengths to convince us why that task IS impossible! If this is the stance we take in our mental processes regarding the solution to a problem, we will be paralyzed by these barriers to the successful solution of this impossible task. We will discover that with this attitude it will literally be impossible to accomplish. And soon we will also discover that someone else has gone ahead and overcome the impossibilities of this task.

The difference between these two mental positions is that one really thinks that it cannot be done, and the other thinks it can. Though that statement may seem to be too simple, it is a fact! An example of this simple truth is the story of when Henry Ford developed the V-8 automobile engine. He had assigned his engineers to build this kind of an engine only to be confronted with the reply: "it couldn't be done!" "It is impossible!" Henry Ford replied that they were to continue working on it until they developed it! A year later they still hadn't overcome the obstacles which they faced. The engineers reported to him that it was a waste of time to continue on this project because it couldn't be done. He told the engineers, "I have decided that I want the V-8 automobile engine, and I always get what I want!" It wasn't long after that comment was heard around the world that the engineers finally broke through the impossibility barrier and produced the object of their search. The result: an engine which produced greater power in less cubic inches than other older engines! Henry Ford exhibited his unusual attitude which put within the reach of the common man an automobile which was affordable and reflected his tenacity which continued to improve that automobile to the point that we can see his admirable mental strength driving along the streets of any city in the world!

Dr. Robert Schuller of the Garden Grove Community Church in Southern California has proved that impossibility tasks can be accomplished through what he calls "possibility thinking." The extent of his ministry proves that many people have accepted this philosophy of possibility thinking and proved that impossible barriers can be overcome. His church ministers to a three part congregation formed of those who attend in the garden part of the auditorium, those in the drive-in section who are able to worship in their cars, and those in the television congregation in many cities across the country. He believes that with God's help he has been able to accomplish great things through possibility thinking.

That we can do the impossible is supported in the teachings of Christ. There are several Scriptures which support this fact. He tells us that "nothing is impossible with God!" "If God be for us, who can be against us?" That key is to BELIEVE that the impossible can be done! The man who says he can and the man who says he can't are reflecting opposite points of belief. One believes he can and goes ahead to prove it, the other is blocked by his unbelief in what he can do. Paul says "I CAN do all things through Christ which strengthens me!" This is the kind of possibility thinking which must be applied to those difficult tasks we face. The powers within the mind are unique in that they will exert great strength in proving the nature of our beliefs. If we believe that we will fail, the mind will assemble a great barrage of reasons why we should fail and with that attitude of our believability set in a negative vein, we will fail. In this limited climate of belief, it will be impossible to achieve all but failure. Napoleon Hill says that no one is ready for a thing until he believes he can acquire it. "The state of mind must be BELIEF, not mere hope or wish!"

With the mind set in a positive vein and claiming the power of God in our desires, the Bible promises that we can achieve "above and beyond all that we can ask or think!" It promises in Mark 9:23 that "everything is possible for a believer!" The unique belief in these cases cannot be in our own powers, but in the inner power given to us by God. Through believing that we CAN achieve we activate this inner power and utilize the power of God in our desires. Remember, God CAN'T do the impossible for us if we doubt what we can do. God is blocked in what He can do for us if we sin by not instinctively having faith in God that He can accomplish above and beyond what we ask. It is one of God's principles that we BELIEVE that we can do the impossible because "with God, all things are possible"!

William James said that: "our belief at the beginning of a doubtful undertaking is the one thing that insures the successful outcome of our venture."

14

THE POWER OF GOAL SETTING

Parkinson's law says that: "A task expands or contracts to the time allotted for it!" If we allow too much time to finish a job, it will take that much time. If we have to get something done quickly the time required for its completion is much less. An example of this is when we get up late for work and we have to hurry to get ready and have breakfast. Usually we seem to be able to hurry fast enough to get everything done so we can just make it to work. We do not allow a leisurely shower and breakfast when we are pressed for time, and take every short cut we can as we drive to work. The task has contracted to the time allotted for it. Conversely, when we wake up earlier than usual we take more time for each preparation task. We may have an extra cup of coffee, and read the paper more thoroughly. We are not as harried as we confront the morning traffic and end up getting to work about the same time as if we had to rush. The task has expanded to the time allotted for it.

This is true in longer range activities as well. If we have a goal set to accomplish a certain long range job which is part of our responsibilities and we allow two months instead of one month, then the task will expand to fit the time of two months instead of the one month in which we may have been able to finish it. "A task expands or contracts to the time allotted for it!"

This concept is also true in goal setting. Setting a goal without a definite target date for its accomplishment is to be tossed to and fro like the waves of the sea. No specific progress is experienced because no specific target is set. How will you know when you get there if you don't know where it is you are supposed to be when you get there? Chet, my father-in-law, has an expression which states this case in a unique way: "if you get there first you make a line—if I get there first, I'll rub it out!" This indefiniteness is a barrier to the realization of specific goals.

It is not enough to state that I want to be president of my company. This goal is too indefinite! The missing factor is a target date. If it weren't that most of us have to be at work at a specific time each morning, we wouldn't get half as much done in business, and the wheels of progress would be flattened on one side.

To set a goal without a target date is to plan without faith that you will ever experience the realization of that goal. The time allotted for the completion of that goal expands into infinity. The Bible states this in James 1:6-7. "But he should ask in faith with never a doubt; [this is saying it is necessary to set a specific date for completion of that goal]. For one who doubts resembles a wave of the sea that is driven and tossed by the wind. Let not that man imagine he will receive anything [his goals] from the Lord."

One who fears setting a specific target date for his goals is evidencing lack of faith in God's ability to help him achieve his goals. When you get your pencil sharpened and begin to figure specifically how much time you feel is necessary to achieve your goals, and then set the date upon which you will realize your goals, you are acting with faith that God is your partner.

Parkinson's Law, Revised

Parkinson's law revised to accommodate the process of reaching goals would be: "Goals expand or contract to the time allotted for them!" One who does not set target dates for his goals never experiences the realization of his desires. He never makes any progress because he hasn't put the principles of success outlined in the Bible behind his statements. He is tossed to and fro like the waves of the sea. His statements reflect: "It sure would be nice if I could some day get to be president!" "I hope that in the near future I will be able to be financially independent!" "Perhaps tomorrow I will go into business for myself!"

These statements are built upon sand and are washed away by the erosion of their indefiniteness. They indicate no specific positional attitude of the mind which sparks the working of the inner power given to us by God. I am told that when a tiger attacks a herd of sheep, he fixes his eye on one specific doomed sheep. As he runs toward that marked animal, others may dart in front of the tiger and are within easy reach of it, but his instincts tell this ferocious attacker that the one he has set his mind upon is the one he is going to get. He keeps his eye on that one sheep and finally achieves his goal. It is not his nature to flit back and forth and try to grab the one temporarily closer to him, but to run toward his target until he achieves it.

The instincts of this animal tell him to set a goal and

to run straight toward it with all of the strength and speed he has. It is unusual for a tiger to miss his mark once he has set his mind upon its goal.

Paul spoke of this singleness of purpose as being essential to proper goal achievement when he wrote in Philippians 3:13, "This one thing I do! Forgetting what is behind and reaching out for what lies before, I push on to the goal...!" Much effort is lost if we encumber ourselves with worthless efforts which do not lead directly towards our goal. If Paul first ran towards his goal and then saw another goal which was closer to him and changed his direction towards the second goal he would lose the momentum which was required in attaining his goal! "This *one* thing I do!" Paul set his sights on the goal which was the propagation of the gospel and that's what he did. He didn't encumber himself in other activities which would drain his valuable energy needed to reach his goal. He ran toward his first and foremost target, and he achieved it.

As a Christian we have an additional advantage when we set goals. Proverbs 16:9 explains that "A man's mind plans his road, but the Lord directs his steps!" Once we set our goals and determine the realistic target date for its attainment, we can depend upon the Lord to direct our steps as He helps us to avoid unnecessary expenditure of energy on misdirected activities. To enjoy this divine help though, it IS necessary to specifically plan what we want and to set a time limit for its attainment. By setting this target date, we can experience the help of the Lord to reach that goal as He directs our steps.

This means that occasionally we WILL have to change our plans in one way or another. Since we cannot see the big picture which is apparent to God in His infinite wisdom, He may direct our steps to avoid dead end streets or activities which will not lead us to our intended goal. As we rely on this promise and let God have His way in directing us, we will experience a much more direct route to our goals than if we had tried to "go it alone." God does direct our steps if we stay in touch with Him and are sensitive to His direction.

As we experience the attainment of our goals we may discover that it is difficult to accomplish a certain phase of reaching that goal. It is not necessary to give up in this task. Instead, we allow God to bring to our mind another way of reaching that phase of the goal. Sometimes it is necessary to wait patiently for God to reveal through new ideas and inspiration a better way to reach our goals. Occasionally it may take longer than we had originally determined for us to reach the goal. We may have miscalculated the target date and discover that we have to set another date. This is all part of the process of reaching goals. But it IS important to have a date set at all times so we will not experience the infinity of dateless goals and the fact that tomorrow never comes.

Once you have begun to realize the power that comes from targeting your goals you will be amazed at how the power within us will work towards the realization of our desires. It is necessary to realize that God makes all good things available for our enjoyment, and that they are ours if we but employ the principles of success contained in the Greatest Success Book of All Time—The Bible.

15

THE ENERGY
TO ACHIEVE SUCCESS

A lot of discussion centers around sources and supplies of energy in this age of ecology. Man, for the first time in the history of the world, is concerned about running out of energy. Efforts are being made to tap the sun as a source of energy. Others tell us that there is a great source of energy in the rise and fall of the ocean's tides. Scientists are now extracting oil from rocks and from the ocean beds. And there are always those who are trying to discover a form of perpetual energy.

Why men do not realize that we already HAVE an inexhaustible source of perpetual energy is difficult to understand. It is necessary to have energy to achieve success. The Bible tells of a source of energy in Philippians 2:13:

"God is the ENERGIZER within you."

And in I Corinthians 12:6:

"There also are varieties of things accomplished, but the same God does all the ENERGIZING in them all."

We have strength and energy we have not even

tapped! We could never deplete this source of energy because it is from an infinite God!

Several places in the Scriptures speak of "the infinite power that works within us." Ephesians 3:20:

> "Now unto Him, who is able with THE POWER THAT WORKS WITHIN US, to do everything, immeasurably far beyond what we pray or think of."

Also in Ephesians 3:16:

> "That He may grant you, in keeping with the wealth of His glory, to be EMPOWERED WITH STRENGTH IN THE INNER SELF by His Spirit."

Is there any doubt that if we appropriate this infinite power we will have a continual, endless supply of strength which is more than equal to any task we set before ourselves?

How Do You Activate this Inner Power?

The Greatest Success Book of all Time provides the key to releasing this inner power in Mark 11:24:

> "Whatever you ask for in prayer, BELIEVE that you have RECEIVED it, and it shall be yours."

BELIEVE that you have RECEIVED! That's the key! We have to BELIEVE that we have already RECEIVED that for which we ask! This simple process activates forces we never were even aware of! It releases the power of God within us to flow freely through us and out of us to affect everyone and everything around us!

BELIEVE that you have RECEIVED it! In this verse the Bible is suggesting that we do the opposite of what one author has labeled as those who are "mental procrastinators" by acting and believing that we already HAVE that for which we pray. This puts our request in the "already happened" category. It is already a fact, not something that may happen in the future. If we believe strongly that we shall receive that for which we ask, then we will be "acting as if it were impossible to fail." We will be acting as though we already have the object of our request.

Mañana

One success book hints that the reason for many people's lack of achievement is that they are "mental proscrastinators." This is someone who puts off everything until "mañana" just as the little fellow did in the song when he said that maybe he wouldn't have to fix the leak in the roof until tomorrow because maybe the rain would go away. These people make indeterminate goals when they say "some day I will be rich." "Some day (in the uncertain future) I will reach my goal." They never chart a specific date in which time they really expect to realize that goal. The mind interprets this "mañana" attitude as though you don't want the success until tomorrow. Since tomorrow never comes, neither does success! The statements of our goals have to be "today" oriented to be effective.

This same book also goes so far as to suggest that if we act like we already have our goal (in a sense, a past tense orientation—it has already happened) that this is an even more powerful command to our subconscious mind of our specific intentions and desires. Is this not what the verse in Mark 11:24 is saying: BELIEVE that you have RECEIVED! The past tense of the word "received" suggests the opposite of the "mañana" philosophy.

William James says that if we "act-as-if" we already had what we ask for, we would get it much sooner. The Bible suggests that we "believe" that we have "received"! Is this not the same as "acting-as-if" we had "received" at our requests?

16

FAITH IS REALITY

One of the first success books ever to appear in print, *Think and Grow Rich* by Napoleon Hill, has a chapter entitled "Thoughts Are Things." In that chapter the author gives credit to the fact that "the man from Nazareth" was the greatest demonstrator of the principle that "thoughts are things." He relates this fact to the demonstration of many miracles performed by Jesus and that these were demonstrations of faith. The Bible confirms this fact to be so in Hebrews 12:1 in which it tells us that thoughts are things and that faith is reality:

> "Faith is the substance [reality] of things hoped for, and the evidence [also reality] of things not seen."

Recall for a moment that everything which has ever been made has as its original form a thought in the mind of a man. The chair in which you are now seated was in its original form a mental thought. The home or office in which you are now reading was originally a thought. The automobile you drive—if it's a Ford— was originally a thought in the mind of Henry Ford. There is not one thing that did not originally exist in the form of a thought seed. Truly, "thoughts are things" and they become reality through the exercise of applied faith.

In many of the miracles that Jesus performed he credited the miracle not only to his miraculous power but to the individual's faith. He helped the individual realize that it was their own faith that healed them. Even today God is ready to help us realize that it is our own faith coupled with the principles in His Word that can help us accomplish our plans.

In Matthew 15:28, the Canaanite woman whose daughter was demon possessed cried to the Lord to help her. The Lord's reply was:

"O woman, your faith is great, be it as you desire."

And from that very moment, her daughter was healed.

Luke 17:11-19 tells us about one of the ten lepers who asked Jesus to heal him. Verse 19 says:

"And he said unto him, arise go thy way, thy faith hath made thee well."

The story in Matthew 9:27-29 talks about the two blind men who asked the Lord to restore their sight. Jesus asked them:

"Do you believe I can do this? They answered Him: Yes, Lord. He then touched their eyes and said: To the measure of your faith it shall be to you."

There are other stories in the Bible that explain that it is according to our faith and the extent to which we believe that we shall receive. James 1:6-8 says:

"But he should ask in faith with never a doubt. For one who doubts resembles a wave of the sea that is driven and tossed by the wind. Let not that man imagine that he will receive anything from the Lord. A double minded man he is, unsteady in all his ways."

Hebrews 11:1 says that "faith is the SUBSTANCE of things hoped for." Faith, of course, is something that we cannot see, but SUBSTANCE is something we can touch and feel and see and recognize as already existing. FAITH IS SUBSTANCE; faith is the thing which we want; faith is believing that we already have our desires; that we have already received that which we have faith in. EVIDENCE in a courtroom is something that the jury can actually look at and analyze. It is the proof of something that we can pick up, hold in our hand and investigate. It is material proof that we already have the object of our faith. That's the kind of belief we can have as this power works within us. When we believe to that extent, then we have already received those things for which we have asked.

God stands ready to empower our faith so that we may accomplish our goals. I Corinthians 2:5 tells us:

"Our faith does not rest on human wisdom
but on divine strength."

17

ACT-AS-IF YOU ARE SUCCESSFUL

Once, when one of my associates and I had been invited to attend a dinner party sponsored by one of our dealers, he made a remark which provoked some thought. We had been in conference all day long and needed to freshen up before attending the evening party. He said: before we go to the party I need to go back to the hotel and "get my act together." He had to get his act together! What a typical statement! It reflects the fact that we are all acting out a role as we participate in the play of life. All of us see ourselves as being a certain type of person and then we set forth to enact that image we hold of ourselves.

Perhaps we see ourselves as a respectable, upright, church-going pillar of the community whose responsibility is to give back to society more than we take from it. If this is your self image then "your act" includes fulfilling that role.

Or, maybe you see yourself as a successful, astute business man without whom your company would not run efficiently. The decisions you make would reflect the fact that you are acting out a successful part in the play of life.

Do you see yourself as "trying to get it together," always aspiring for the cherished level of success which denotes that person who has made it? Success will be here tomorrow, but, alas, tomorrow never comes!

Your self image may be that of one who just can't seem to do anything right! You try and try, but nothing goes right for you. Your self concept has been beat down by external influences to such a point that you consider yourself to be a failure!

These are only a few of the roles which people may play. We all play some kind of role as we experience life. Perhaps you have never realized this fact, but it is true. Stop right now and try to determine what kind of role you are playing. Are you satisfied with it? Is it bringing you the fulfillment you seek? Or, do you wish you could change it to something else?

You can change it to conform with whatever you wish. Or if you like whatever role you are presently enacting, you can enhance it to give it greater depth and additional perspective! It's up to you to determine what you wish to become.

A powerful success book entitled *Wake Up And Live* written by Dorothea Brand suggests that you "act-as-if it's impossible to fail." If you are a failure, according to your standards, "act-as-if it's *impossible* to fail" in each task you undertake. Act as if you are an outstanding success in all that you do and cannot fail. You have heard of those who touch something and it turns to gold. They act in such a way that they expect everything to turn to gold. They perform their duties in such a way that they expect to be successful. As a result of their method of acting, they are successful!

Uncle Jim was that kind of man. When he started as

an office boy, with the Hartford Fire Insurance Company as a youngster of eighteen, no one realized that he would some day be the President of the Reno, Nevada office!

As a result of his success, he invested heavily in real estate and ultimately became a millionaire. He made money in everything he did. The story is told of the time he bought some cheap property outside of town for several thousand dollars for his horses to run on. It was only a year later that he was contacted by a group of businessmen who wanted to buy that very parcel. Jim didn't want to sell it because then he wouldn't have a place for his horses to graze!

The men insisted that he name a price for the property because they wanted it so badly. He calculated that if he named a high enough price that perhaps he could get rid of them and they wouldn't bother him anymore about the property!

He had only paid about $3000 for the property a year earlier, so he reasoned that if he named ten times what he paid for it, or $30,000 they would get off of his back about buying it.

Upon hearing of this price for this desired property, however, the businessmen reached for their checkbook and filled it out to the tune of $30,000! Everything Jim did turned to gold! Why? Because he thought these kind of successful thoughts!

The Bible confirms this concept in Romans 13:13 when it suggests that we "act as befits the daytime." In this passage it uses several examples of those things we should avoid: carousing, drinking, prostitution, debauchery, quarrelling and jealousy—all of which are negative acts. It explains that we should act as befits the daytime. Daytime represents those positive qualities which will lead to successful living. It is saying we should act-as-if it were impossible to fail by avoiding those negative activities which inevitably lead to failure.

You may ask: "Why should I act successful if I am really not?" The reason you consider yourself unsuccessful is because you have been doing unsuccessful things. You have been acting as if it were POSSIBLE to fail. BELIEVE that you can be successful by acting successfully and things will change miraculously!

You have the power to choose success or failure, and that choice is reflected in the decision to either act successfully or as a failure. The results of either choice will follow as night follows day. It is up to you to "get your act together!"

18

DON'T LOOK BACK UNLESS
THAT'S THE WAY YOU WANT TO GO

Someone else phrased it with a different slant: "Don't look back because something might be gaining on you!" We all remember what happened to Lot's wife when she violated this success principle and what a salty individual she became!

Paul the Apostle phrased it more positively: "Forgetting those things which are behind, let us press forward!"

Dwelling on the "good old days" is to live in the past and to exhibit a negative, limiting philosophy. It is a positive individual manifesting faith in the power of God who "presses forward!" Pressing forward is to believe that you can achieve through your inner power. It is displaying an I CAN belief that God will direct your paths onward and upward to great heights of success.

Looking back is evidence of fear. Fear of the future, fear of the challenges of new horizons, fear that you won't be able to respond to new ways to use your talents and abilities.

It is nature's law that if we don't exercise our physical muscles they will dry up, and we will eventually

NOT be able to use them. Not using our mental muscles by moving forward will cause our attitudes to decay. This is why the Bible challenges us to "daily renew our mental attitude." When was the last time you entertained a new idea? Have you ever tried to consider new and more efficient methods of accomplishing your tasks? Columbus thought a new thought when he said the world was round and look what happened because of his forward looking thought! Columbus may have been inspired to his historic journey by the fact that the Bible told us 2000 years ago that the world is round in Isaiah 40:22 in which verse it speaks of the "circle of the earth."

Let us forget those mistakes we have made which place a backward drag on us and begin acting with an attitude of faith in our abilities and keep believing and expecting to achieve success. A successful person makes more mistakes than the person who is a failure! But it takes only one success to be successful. A person can experience many failures in their lives and then experience one success and be a "successful" individual. One success makes a person successful, but one failure does not make a person a failure! However, if you stop short of that one success by looking back then you still are a failure and may be thinking: "I tried it and failed, therefore I guess I'm a failure." You're exhibiting the attitude of reverse vision and of concentrating on your mistakes rather than your successes. You're not exercising an attitude of belief and faith in your abilities, since faith is not instinctive in the things that you do. You're condemning yourself to failure by entertaining doubts.

Only through considered study of the success principles found in the Scriptures can you discover your own personal application of the success principles through which to move forward to great heights of accomplishment!

19

VISUALIZATION OF SUCCESS

It would seem to be an apparent fact that most people would choose success over failure. Little thought would be necessary to decide that a successful status in any endeavor is better than failure. There are many reasons why there are more failures than successes; however, one major reason stands out. That reason is that many people dwell on reasons which cause failure instead of those factors which would contribute to their success. They contemplate reasons which justify their failure rather than concentrate on why they should succeed in their activities.

A phrase in a song in the musical South Pacific says: "If you don't have a dream, how can you have a dream come true?" There is a multitude of stories of those young dreamers in school who became fantastic successes. Everyone thought that they were merely day dreamers. But some dreamt of "going to the moon" and eventually they went there!

Psychologists inform us that the human mind can't tell the difference between a real and a vividly imagined situation. If we dream vividly of being successful in a venture our mind interprets this as a suggestion that this is what we desire. Since we become what we think about (as a man thinks, so is he) if we vividly imagine something we tend to become or attract to us the nature of those thoughts.

That many people experience failure is due to the fact that they give more mental energy to considering where they have been in terms of unacceptable conditions which have yielded failure than they do in creating the success conditions of prosperity. If most people want to be successful. why do they dwell on their past failures? "Forgetti. ॒ those things which are behind, I press on...."

Since our mind attracts to us the conditions similar to the nature of our thoughts, if we dwell on past problems, we will attract similar future problems. We can change our future, however, by changing what we think about. Dwell on thoughts which reflect those conditions you wish to experience. A guided missile is programmed to hit the mark. Missing it is not ᴄ a part of its programming. We should program our tⅈⅈⅈnking to hit the mark of success and never recognize the possibility of failing.

By dwelling only on those thoughts of success we too can be assured of hitting the mark. Failure will not be a factor!

When we dwell on successful thoughts, we use a technique to more indelibly impress our subconscious mind with the goals we wish to achieve. That technique is to form a MENTAL PICTURE of the success we wish to achieve. Since the mind cannot tell the difference between a real and a vividly imagined situation, we can vividly form a mental picture of the conditions we wish to assume in our life.

The Bible confirms this unique fact of the human mind. In Matthew 5:28 it records: "Whoever looks on a woman to lust after her has committed adultery with her already in his heart." To think vividly about a situation is the same as actually experiencing it in the mind! The mind cannot tell the difference between a real and a vividly imagined situation.

A game that young children occasionally play when "initiating" another child into their club is to blindfold the new member and inform him that he has to be "branded with a hot iron" to become a full fledged member. What happens is that as the child is led into the room which has the hot iron ready for the branding procedure, he is asked to sit down in a chair and is then blindfolded. At this point, he is expecting something very painful to occur as part of the initiation ceremony. What actually happens, however, is that instead of using the actual hot iron, the members use an ice cube which they touch to the arm. As this is done, they put the tip of the hot iron into a nearby bowl of water. As the hissing sound emanates from the hot iron interacting with the cold water the ice cube is placed against the arm. The body cannot tell immediately whether this is a hot or cold object which is touching it. However, because the initiate saw the hot iron, he assumes that he has been properly branded. Stories have been told that in some cases, the situation was so real that blisters have occurred on the arm!

Another situation illustrating this same thing is about a hypnotist who when taking a cold tablespoon and placing it on the arm can cause blisters because he has told the individual that this is a hot branding iron which is being placed on the arm.

The mind acts in the same way when we continually see ourselves as a failure, and that we can't do anything right. The subconscious will use every bit of its strength to prove to us that we are right and we will continue to be a failure if this is the information that we continually feed it. "As a man thinks in his mind, so is he!"

Therefore, if we vividly imagine conditions of success, our mind will accept these thoughts as the conditions we wish to create and will set about attracting those success conditions. "Whatever you sow, that will you also reap!"

The importance of visualization is spoken of in Proverbs 29:18. "Where there is no vision, the people run wild." A torpedo without a goal (a vision of its target) will run wild. It will not know where to go. Our mind works in the same way. If we lack a clear vision of what we want to accomplish we will run wild. We will be tossed to and fro like a wave of the sea—always moving, but never accomplishing anything or getting anywhere. The Bible calls this kind of person a "double-minded man." "Let not that man imagine he will receive anything from the Lord because he is unstable in all his ways."

By assigning to our mind a clear mental vision of what we wish to achieve, the power within us will work for us to achieve the success conditions of our goal in an effortless manner. But it will not work unless we have a clear picture of our goal in mind. An unfocused camera cannot yield a clear picture. A mind which is unfocused will yield confusion and frustration.

Dwell upon the clear vivid picture of the success you desire. You will discover things happening FOR you instead of TO you!

20

AGREEMENT OF PURPOSE

Several success books discuss the principle involving the combining of two people's thought processes in a cooperative effort which produce greater results than would be achieved thinking separately. Napoleon Hill explains that it is almost like a third mind was present when two people are thinking strongly on any given subject.

The Bible supports this concept when it recorded many years ago in Matthew 18:19:

> "I assure you that if two of you are agreed
> on earth about anything for which you pray,
> it will be done for you by My Heavenly
> Father. For where two or three have gath-
> ered in My Name, I am there with them."

In this type of cooperative effort we know that the third mind is that of the Lord Jesus Christ—the mind of God is present in the midst of these two or three who are gathered for a common purpose.

In the second world war a process was developed which used this principle and was called "brainstorming." The name suggests the idea of actually "storming" the brain for ideas. It works by requesting a group of people who are knowledgeable on a particular subject to present any and all solutions to a problem which may flash into their minds. These ideas are recorded for later evaluation. One important principle in the process of brainstorming is that as they are meeting together and expecting ideas to come that no one person condemns or judges the ideas of another. To condemn anyone else's idea would inflict a negative force which would inhibit the creative process in the flow of any new ideas. Whereas, if a positive atmosphere is continually present, one mind will spark another for a new idea that may not have been thought of without the brainstorming process.

An illustration of an idea that came forth from one of these sessions happened during World War II. It seems that aircraft designers were having trouble in figuring out how to extricate fighter pilots from a burning or disabled fighter plane fast enough before the plane exploded in mid-air. Too many pilots were lost as they scrambled to get out of it before it exploded.

One member of a brainstorming team suggested that the pilot could be "shot out of the plane." At first thought, this may have seemed like a ridiculous idea, because how would you shoot a pilot out of a plane? But, the rules were strictly adhered to in this session and no one judged the idea negatively. Another individual saw the potential in that idea and grasped it by adding, "yes, that's a good idea because we can put him in an enclosed compartment and then literally shoot the entire compartment out of the plane which can descend by parachute safely to the ground.

This is an illustration of the power of many minds which are cooperating towards a common goal. The Bible suggests in the passage in Matthew that where two or three are gathered for a common purpose, that

God is there in the midst, providing that these people AGREE and do not condemn any one idea through disagreement or arguing.

There may be a specific law as to the extent to which creativity is engendered when two or more people are gathered together. I suggest an illustration which may help. One person is capable of a specific given amount of thought depending upon his believability and expectancy. Two people are capable of more than twice the amount of thought that they would be able to generate if they were thinking as separate individuals. It is similar to using an illustration of a pipe which carries water. A one inch pipe carries a given volume of water. A two inch pipe would logically seem to carry twice the amount of water carried by the one inch pipe, but a two inch pipe carries FOUR times as much water as the one inch pipe. A four inch pipe carries eight times as much water as a one inch pipe, etc.

Another way to illustrate this is found in comparing the volume of a one inch circle and a two inch circle. The two inch circle has four times the area of a one inch circle.

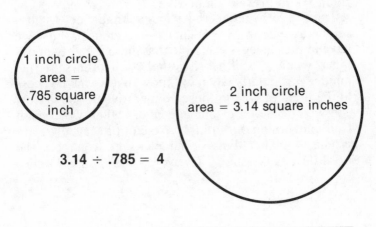

1 inch circle
area =
.785 square
inch

2 inch circle
area = 3.14 square inches

3.14 ÷ .785 = 4

Alexander Graham Bell once said: "Great discoveries and improvements invariably involve the cooperation of many minds." I believe that some day we may know exactly the amount of creativity which may be released by the cooperation of two minds who believe together and look to God as their source for answers to specific requests.

The Bible does not limit us to the kinds of things for which we can ask in these cooperative sessions. It says that if we agree on any one thing, that it shall be done for us. These can be answers to problems that we face. A husband and wife can kneel together and thereby form an alliance of two minds working together for a common purpose through God's help. It can be two business partners working together. It can be two school children working together to solve a homework problem. It can be a lay member and his pastor working cooperatively to solve a spiritual problem. It can be a request for creativity or for new ideas for solutions to business or personal problems. There is no limit that God makes upon this particular process. We can use it in any area of our life and expect solutions to present themselves.

The Proverbs tell us that "in an abundance of counselors there is safety." What a tremendous promise we have in this success principle that there is safety in our ideas when we gather together with others of like minds, particularly when we know that we have access to the mind of God in these cooperative periods. How can we fail in any of our endeavors when we consult God concerning our affairs? We can't because we are promised that "Man's mind plans his road but the Lord directs his steps" (Proverbs 16:9).

21

STRESS VS. SUCCESS

The accepted interpretation of success indicates that a balance of several factors are necessary. Success in financial matters without accompanying good health would leave the degree of success attainment open to question. Adjustment in one's personal life and in his understanding of himself is certainly an important factor in one's achievement of a success standing, but when the wolf is at the door along with these circumstances, the validity of his personal adjustment is subject to examination!

We have all read stories of successful individuals of those who have climbed to a high pinnacle of success in their fields of endeavor only to read in the newspaper that they have jumped out of the fortieth floor window to escape the pressure of success. Pressurized success, that is, success under stressful conditions is open to severe criticism.

I recall a visit to a dermatologist who made a remark reflective of questionable success. During our conversation I remarked that I had learned how to relieve the stress of daily living, and that I never got uptight about problems! This is part of my personal testimony that the Greatest Success Book of All Time—The Bible—

teaches a way of escape from stressful conditions exerted upon us in our business and personal life. The doctor indicated an urgent interest in my remarks when he said: "maybe I am the one who should be on the examining table rather than you!" Though financially successful as a doctor, he was looking for a way to relieve the stress of daily living.

The attainment of success is dependent upon progressively moving towards certain predetermined goals. We are conditioned in this way from the time we are born. We are first taught the basic needs of life such as potty training, learning to eat without making a mess, learning to dress ourselves, tie our shoes, etc. These are some of our first levels of accomplishment which are expected of us. We enter school and learn that we cannot remain in kindergarten, but must progress. As we continue into college, we discover that to become a "professional student"—to remain in college for an excessively long period and never entering the world of applying that knowledge—is frowned upon

We are expected to advance in business to higher levels of responsibility, to accomplish more and to contribute to society in increasing levels. All of these demands create stress, which can build to a danger point and cause us to become ineffective in all of our endeavors. Yet few seek active ways of dealing in an appropriate way with stress. In fact, many people, in their efforts to cope with pressure, actually use the negative principle. You may have heard the remark: "I am under such unbearable pressure that I don't know what I am going to do!" That's a negative statement if I ever heard one, and is responsible for creating an even greater problem because "by your words you are condemned and by your words you are set free!" These words condemn this person to an even more severe sentence imposed by his stressful living. The mind reacts in an appropriate manner to those ideas and thoughts presented to it through our words. We are either condemned or set free by their vast power!

Before you jump to conclusions and feel that my suggestions to you to handle stress successfully is to merely say that "I am not under pressure and feel quite relaxed," let me assure you that the Bible includes specific suggestions which may be applied in a positive way to handle stress conditions. These success principles may be used to produce a low key attitude indicative of a calm, relaxed and well adjusted life style.

There are many techniques offered which lead to a release of stress: meditation; hypnosis; psychiatry; prayer—all with certain specific results. Dr. Herbert Benson recognized the problem of stress in his book *The Relaxation Response.* He noted that the body offers a way of dealing with the build up of tension. The book offers a dynamic and successful way of dealing with the common problem of tension.

Years ago the Bible spoke of the stress problem in Psalm 40:1-3.

> "I waited and waited for the Lord; then He bent over to me and heard my cry. He brought me up from a destructive pit, from the miry clay, and set my feet on a rock, steadying my steps. He put a new song in my mouth, a praise to our God!"

David explained that he had fallen into the destructive pit (literal translation: noisy pit) which imprisons one under the bondage of tension. He also exclaimed that the Lord had allowed him to escape these chains when he wrote: "He lifted me up from the miry clay." How apt are those words because how intensely stressful living can bog us down in the miry and sticky clay of urgent problems!

There are many conditions of normal life which need to be relieved, such as hunger pains. Think of how uncomfortable life would be if we could not relieve this problem. Several times each day we take specific measures to eliminate the prodding of hunger pangs by sitting down to a delicious meal.

When a low reading on the thermometer causes us to be cold, we put on warmer clothing to relieve this problem. When we are hot, we turn on the air cooler. Why then, do we not successfully deal with the problem of stress? Perhaps, because you have heard your mother offer this injunction on a cold day: "Now son, put your coat on before you go outside," but never this warning: "Be certain to relax if you begin to get uptight!" We are not taught to deal with stress until we experience the pain of ulcers. It is unfortunate that one of the most popular cures for ulcers caused by stress is the doctor's knife.

We are not suggesting that ulcers may be cured through the techniques offered in succeeding pages. The doctor is the one who has to attend to this severe problem. Our suggestion is that the CONDITIONS which cause ulcers may be alleviated through these unstressing techniques discussed in this chapter.

How did David solve his problem of stress? He waited upon the Lord! In fact, he exclaimed that he waited and waited for the Lord and "then he heard me and lifted me up" from the stressful conditions of life. Certainly if anyone had problems, it was David. He had King Saul chasing him; problems with Bathsheba, wars to fight, and a giant to face! Few of us can testify of problems so magnanimous as this, yet, many of us have difficulty in successfully coping with life! Why? Because we do not take steps to eliminate the early signs of the ugliness of tension.

Several years ago I was the marketing manager of an international firm and worked directly with the Chairman of the Board. His management technique included continually piling additional responsibilities upon an individual so that the only way to handle all of the work was to work during lunch hours and evenings. It was my choice to respond to these responsibilities to the best of my time and abilities, but there was a great potential for stress to enter into this schedule. It often did impose itself upon my attitude and could have destroyed any chance to successfully accomplish my responsibilities.

I utilized a technique for cancelling the potential of stress by reminding myself that "I can only do what I can do, and I will begin working on the one project which I deemed to be most important." I would continue by reasoning that: "I am calm and relaxed now as I approach this first task, and I will remain calm and composed as I continue to discharge my duties!"

David meditated on the Lord on a daily basis, and found release from tension. He actually established a quiet time during which he allowed the strength of the Lord to "renew his mental attitude!" (Ephesians 4:23).

Many of the meditation and relaxation schools of thought proclaim that we need several quiet periods each day during which to allow our mental energies to recharge themselves. Most of these meditation techniques suggest a twenty minute period in the morning and one at night during which the mind blanks out any outside thoughts which may encumber the mental processes. The Bible suggests that the morning is an excellent time to engage in our first meditation period (Psalms 5:1-3). It also speaks of communion with the Lord during the night seasons (Psalms 16:7). My wife tells me that when she awakens during the night she often has a precious time of meditation upon the things of the Lord.

It is necessary during these meditation periods that we allow our mind to be totally free from the daily cares and responsibilities we face. The Bible speaks of a time during which we "wait" on the Lord. It also explains that often our spirit communes with the Holy Spirit. It is during these times of spiritual communion that I receive much inner strength and release from stress. But, if we are continually talking or actively thinking during the meditation periods, how can the Spirit of God commune with us and how can we be renewed with strength from on high?

It is most effective to practice these meditation periods in a comfortable position in a chair or on the bed, where we can then totally relax and receive the needed strength.

The question may arise that it is wonderful to relax in the morning and again at night, but I get uptight during the day at my office and I cannot practice these relaxation methods under these conditions! I heartily answer: "Yes you can benefit from these meditation techniques at work!" There is a combination of methods which you may employ to your relaxed benefit. Two separate success principles which, when combined, produce a powerful technique which will benefit you all day long. The two have already been mentioned in this chapter, but now let's consider how to use them to their optimum advantage!

Once you have established the practice of meditating every day (well, almost every day) you extend the benefit of these quiet moments throughout the remainder of the day. How? By reminding yourself through directive words (remember the power of words which we talked about earlier in this chapter). When stressful circumstances seek to enter into your attitude, simply remind yourself that "you are relaxed and are not in the habit of getting uptight!" The benefits derived from the two twenty minute meditation periods will extend into the responsibilities you face each day as a result of this programming statement. Program your mental computer that you are calm and composed and that you do not respond to stressful thoughts. As you condition yourself with these ideas, bring into focus in your mind a picture of your meditation period that morning and how relaxed you felt during that quiet time. The combination of the appropriate words and restful scene in your mind will act as a healing balm for any trouble you feel in your soul.

It is important that you immediately "bring into captivity" any negative thought which would engender a stressful response which may pop into your attitude. If you do not immediately eliminate these thoughts when they appear, they may germinate and take root in your attitude and you will have more that just a simple seed to cast out. You will have to tear away at your attitude to extricate the damage done by the roots hooking themselves into your mind.

A calm and relaxed attitude is a habit which is well adjusted and mature. It comes through practicing these success principles on a daily basis. Hebrews 5:14: "But solid food is for the mature, for those whose faculties [attitude] have been trained *by practice* to distinguish between good and evil."

22

LOSING MENTAL
(AND OTHER) WEIGHT

A story is told about a unique weight loss plan which really produced results! Two individuals were exchanging views about this popular subject when one of them remarked to the other: "I can show you a way to lose those thirty pounds you claim that you can't lose, but you'll have to do exactly as I say!" The other man replied, "I'll do almost anything to lose this extra weight I have been carrying around!" "That's the point," replied the first man, "you have been carrying it around needlessly! Do what I say and you'll lose it quickly!"

"What is it I have to do? Do I have to eat special foods, or take some weight loss pills, or exercise furiously? These I have already done and I still don't lose!" The first man said, "No, it isn't anything like that!" "Well, tell me quickly what I have to do?"

Before I explain what the layman's prescription was, let me add that though this system worked for this overweight person, we are not recommending it without the guidance of a qualified physician.

The first man secured some handcuffs which were attached to two fifteen pound suitcases and then attached to each of the man's wrists. He was then instructed: "wear these cases for two weeks and do not remove them at any time!"

He had to wear them while he ate, worked, slept, showered, shaved and drove his car. He soon began to realize what the magnitude of the extra weight he was carrying with him was on his body. Each time he reached for an unneeded sweet roll he felt that extra weight tugging at his arm. The need for weight loss was quite short in its arrival! He quickly slimmed down to a longer and more trim life.

There is a spiritual and mental message in this story. Thirty extra pounds can be an enormous drag to your physical potential the same as any mental load can drag an individual down to a dull and drab existence! Many Christians are dragging extra weight around with them by bearing the weight of their own guilt. This unnecessary load acts as an impediment to their success potential.

I John 3:21 bears out this concept: "loved ones, IN CASE OUR HEARTS DO NOT CONDEMN US, then we draw near to God with confidence, and whatever we may ask we receive from Him!" You can ask for what you want. "In case your hearts [attitude, mind, emotions, guilt] do not condemn you." Now why would someone condemn themselves? Because of the guilt they may carry with them because of unforgiven sin! They feel they don't deserve to be successful and are not living up to their potential achievement level.

I can remember the days when my heart severely condemned me down deep in my soul. Satan injected this type of thought in my mind: "it would be nice to be able to ask God for whatever you want, but I know that I don't deserve to receive it because of sin in my life, so why should I ask?'' My heart was condemning me and thereby cancelled the potential receipt of anything from the Lord! This is a horribly depleting feeling with which to struggle and which will stop the possibilities of any success achievement towards the abundant life!

Why would someone condemn themselves? In my case, it was because I hadn't appropriated the total message of forgiveness extended to me through Jesus Christ. I hadn't forgiven myself of my wrongdoings! Christ had forgiven me, but I hadn't yet done so, and because of that problem, my heart subconsciously condemned me!

John 3:17 tells us that God didn't send his Son to condemn the world but that through Him it could be saved! Romans 8:1 promises us that there is no condemnation to those in Christ Jesus! Some people are so desperately confronted with the extra spiritual and mental weight of their self-condemnation that they need a psychiatrist to help relieve them! Though a Christian psychiatrist can be of tremendous assistance in an individual's personal growth program, he cannot forgive sin! However, he can point out that they can receive forgiveness by appropriating the success principle found in the Greatest Success Book of All Time—The Bible!

My own experience in this situation was unique because I had heard of this message all of my life. It wasn't until its content passed from the intellectual understanding of this principle to the quiet emotional application that I began to receive answers to my prayers!

I recorded on tape these principles of receiving total forgiveness of sin and of not being condemned by God and then listened to them over and over so I could achieve the real impact of this vitally important success message in my life. When it finally hit that through Christ I was the same as if I'd never sinned, I felt a welcome release of mental weight which was acting as a drag to my potential success, and in its place came an enormous surge of inner power that impelled me to set goals I had never thought possible before!

Satan wants to keep us in a state of spiritual deprivation by reminding us that because of sin in our life we can't expect God to hear our prayers! Many Christians accept this story as the truth into which they become locked, when the Gospel of Christ proclaims a complete forgiveness and total availability of an endless supply of power and energy through which we can do all things *immeasurably far beyond which we ask or think!"*

23

PERSONAL POWER FOR SUCCESS

Whenever I speak to sales organizations on the subject of motivation I explain that selling, like life, is a game. It is a game in which some will win and others will lose. Selling is a unique game, however, since either both parties win or both parties lose! How's that? Either the customer and the salesman both win or they both lose! If the salesman fails to convince the customer that they should purchase the product and they walk out of the store without having bought, the customer loses the benefits of owning the product and the conveniences and pleasure which he may have derived from its use. And the salesman loses, because he didn't receive the fun and satisfaction of getting the customer to act immediately in terms of buying it today—and he also lost the pleasure of receiving a commission from making another sale!

However, if the customer had bought the product they would have won the pleasure of its use along with the convenience which it would have added to their life. The salesman also would have won because of the satisfaction he would have received from influencing the customer to take action immediately, and also in terms of receiving a commission from the sale. Either both win or both lose in a selling situation.

This is also true in the game of life. If you give up in your pursuit to achieve your goals, you lose the satisfaction of achieving significantly in your endeavors. You lose the pleasure of knowing that you have contributed to society in a manner which will benefit others to make their life better. There may also be a financial loss which may have accrued to you if you had won. However, if you win in the game of life, you score in many ways. The contentment which will be yours knowing that you are doing your part to make this a better world in which to live; the sharing of your experiences of achieving success with others to help them find their way, and also the benefits derived from the higher level of life that you will be experiencing as a result of your success. You win in many ways, and so do many others!

Each person has a certain amount of energy, whether mental or physical, with which to do any job. This energy increases as you become more involved in your work, or it dissipates with disuse. I discovered this to be true when I decided to add another room and a triple car port to our house in Tucson, Arizona. Though I had done this kind of work before, it had been several years before and I was really physically out of shape. That became apparent to me when I actually got started in the building process itself! I wasn't able to put in a full day of work at first because I just didn't have enough energy. This fact was emphasized after several days of work when my right elbow began to give me excessive pain. After an examination by the doctor, he explained to me that I had "tennis elbow"! I told him that this was pretty ridiculous because I hadn't been playing tennis recently. After a good laugh, he explained that this is just a term which describes what happens to tennis players when they play too hard. He continued by telling me that since I hadn't used a hammer for quite a while, the excessive use of the elbow caused the same problem experienced by tennis players. After some medication and several days of rest I was able to return to my building plans.

In several weeks, I was in good shape and approached the task with plenty of energy and enthusiasm. In fact, the longer I worked each day on the project, the more energy I seemed to have, because this kind of work is fun to me. It was quite a change from the daily responsibilities I have in training and lecturing and was an opportunity to get some physical exercise. I actually lost four inches on the waist as a result of this addition to the house.

It is a fact that the more you use your energy and enthusiasm in approaching any job set before you, the more you will have to use on future endeavors! It is like any muscle of the body. If you exercise it through use, you will be able to continue to use it and the more you exercise it the more it will assist you in performing your duties. However, if you let it shrivel up from disuse, you will eventually not be able to use it!

I usually explain to sales organizations that as a salesman each one has a certain amount of selling energy with which to approach each sales presentation. A customer also has a certain amount of energy to contribute to the interchange between the salesman and customer. This is their buying energy that they use when considering a certain product and asking questions about it. It is a simple fact, I always explain to them, that the person who runs out of his energy first loses the deal! If you, as a sales person, run out of your selling energy before the customer runs out of their buying energy, you lose! However, if you hang in there in the sales presentation with enthusiasm, you will begin to discover new reserves of power and energy that you never knew you had available before.

Application of the other success principles in this book will help you to realize this added power. One of these is to expect to make the sale! When you approach the selling situation really expecting to make the sale, you receive great sources of energy with which to reach your sales goal! Without the faith of expectancy in a selling situation, it can become a most discouraging experience. If you secretly harbor the doubt that you don't expect to make this sale, your lack of self-confidence and depleted supply of energy will disappoint you in your ability to finally convince the customer of the merits of your product.

This is not only true in the selling situation, but also in each of life's experiences. Your wife and children will not have proper respect for you if you approach the family living situation with an anemic attitude exhibiting a lack of self-confidence in your ability to exercise the responsibilities of a father. However, as the leader of the family, if you demonstrate an enthusiasm for life and its problems and challenges and have energy and wisdom with which to solve each one, you will powerfully lead each family member on to the dynamic experiences of life.

"Faith without works is dead" is God's pointed message to us in this regard. "Use it or lose it" is the way Charles E. (Tremendous) Jones puts it in his book *Life is Tremendous*. Matthew 13:12 declares: "For whoever has shall receive superabundantly, but whoever has not shall be deprived of whatever he has." Let's paraphrase that verse. "Whoever has the sense to use what energy and abilities he already has (no matter how much or little) will receive superabundantly more than he already has. He that does not use the talents he has been given will discover that the little he already has is slipping away from him." The only way to gain more personal power for success is to prove your faith by getting into the ballpark and playing the game with all your might! Proverbs 14:23 records: "In all toil there is profit, but mere talk leads only to want."

24

THE POTENTIAL "IDEA"
OF SUCCESS

A story is told about two nations who were at war in the Medieval years and an unusual tactic used by one of the Kings. One of the generals raced up to him to explain that the "other side" now had the ultimate weapon! "Well, tell me about it," said the King. The general breathlessly reported that he wasn't quite sure just what kind of new weapon it was that they had, but that he had heard that it was capable of inflicting great harm upon our troups. He told him that the enemy could hide in the hills on the other side of the river and that this weapon could shoot a great destructive force more than several miles. They wouldn't be able to tell where it was coming from nor when they were going to shoot it. The whole thing was terrible because the general had no way in which to combat this formidable weapon!

The King could tell that the general was really disturbed by the potential force of the enemy. He also sensed that the general was more frightened by the fear of this unknown and strange weapon than he was of the potential damage that it might do to his men.

The King demonstrated that he was a wise ruler in

the advice that he gave to the general. He realized that until they were sure that the enemy really had such a formidable weapon that the only thing that they had to contend with was the "idea" of that weapon. They were not sure that the enemy even had such a terrible destructive device, and until they could be certain of that fact, they were only fighting an "idea"! However, a negative idea such as this one can be just as detrimental to winning as the physical evidence of a powerful weapon can be—if you let it have its power to affect you!

The wise King knew that the only way he could instill confidence in the mind of the general that they could handle whatever the enemy could do to them was to tell the general about an even more powerful weapon that we now have—even if it wasn't yet ready to be used. The King knew that since the enemy's weapon was still only an idea in the general's mind, that he would have to come up with an even more powerful IDEA with which to fight the enemy's idea.

Most of our battles are not fought with physical weapons but in the realms of mental images (ideas) in our mind. If we believe a certain fact about ourselves to be true, it will eventually evidence itself in our life, whether that fact is true or untrue, positive or negative. (As a man thinks in his heart, so is he!) When that general was convinced by the wise King that he had a better weapon with which to combat the enemy, that produced a mental image in his mind with which he could influence his troups to fight harder and longer and win the battle. It was the IDEA of the better weapon that won, not the weapon itself. The Ford Motor Company certainly realizes this. For many years their advertising theme has been: "Ford has a better idea!"

Occasionally, when medical doctors realize that a psychosomatically ill patient actually has no physical ailment plaguing him, a simple, little blue (or yellow) sugar pill is a strong enough "idea" to cure him. Because the patient believes strongly enough in the advice of the doctor and in the power of the sugar pill to cure him, the patient is made well. The patient, of course, didn't know that the only ingredient in his "magic" pill was sugar. It is not the pill that cured him, of course, but his faith in the doctor's recommendation that he takes this pill "three times a day" until the condition goes away. The doctor has used a simple "idea" to cure the patient.

The Bible concurs in this when the Lord recommended to one of his followers after he had cured him of his leprosy that he "tell no man." The man had expressed his faith in Jesus' ability to heal him by exclaiming: "Lord, if you are willing you are able to cleanse me." This was a demonstration of positive faith in Jesus' ability to heal him.

An idea may be negative as well. When the witch doctors in dark Africa put a spell on someone they are usually afflicted with the curse. This is negative faith. Jesus realized that though the leper believed positively in his ability, that if he had gone out and told everyone that the Lord had cured him, they might have induced a negative effect upon the cured man by saying something like this: "You might think that you are cured, but it is only the emotional effect you are experiencing of being around such a powerful figure like Jesus! Tomorrow you will still be a leper, you just wait and see!" This is a negative idea which could potentially have just as powerful effect in a damaging way upon the man as did Jesus' cure. Therefore, Jesus knew that this could be a potential problem if he told everyone about it, so he told him to "tell no man!"

Walter M. Germain explained it this way in his book *The Magic Power of Your Mind:* The leper's believability "may easily be dampened by a storm of ridicule. The Supraconscious level of the (leper's) mind, ever amenable to control by the power of suggestion, is adversely influenced by an unfavorable attitude (of those unbelievers). Without being consciously aware of it, the individual loses faith."

The potential power of an idea may be applied to other situations as well. Proverbs declares: "Do not boast about tomorrow for you do not know what a day will bring forth." Again, this is a positive idea which is designed to avoid the potential negative problems of telling others about your intended plans. Let's take an example. Suppose you have a fantastic idea for a new product which would save much work on the part of housewives. You really believe in the idea and want to market it so others may benefit from it. However, there are a few simple problems which you have to work out yet, and you are involved in solving these problems. From your experiments on the product, you are convinced that you will be able to construct a working model of this idea which you can demonstrate to those who are able to build and market such a product.

Because of your excitement for the potential of this product, you discuss it, in kind of a boastful manner, with others. They coldly inform you that "my uncle tried something like that and when he showed it to some manufacturers, they stole the idea from him, and he got nothing as a result of all of his work while the manufacturers are still making millions on it!" Wow! What a negative idea! How much power this negative statement can have upon the future potential success of a powerful idea like the product you have been working on! The Bible says: "tell no man!"

When you prematurely share your idea with the wrong people, you divide the potential power in that idea by inflicting another (potentially more powerful) idea upon it before your original idea has a chance to be nurtured by the sunshine of your faith and belief in its potential. However, if you keep that idea to yourself and discuss the plans only with the Lord, you receive infinite wisdom and guidance with which to properly develop and promote it and who knows to what extent it will benefit everyone that uses that product! If, when you decide to plant carrots, you prematurely share the product of your efforts with others by pulling it up to determine whether or not it is properly growing, you will have nothing to show for your efforts at the proper time of full development. However, if you wait to share your produce with others until the correct harvest time, you will have a fully developed product to deliver!

The Proverbs record: "Let another praise you, and not your own mouth; a stranger, and not your own lips." If you prematurely talk about something that you are working on, you divide your power to continue working on it and find that the potential value of that idea dwindles away just as water down the drain. It can never be retrieved! "Tell no man!"

25

YOU MAY DESIGN
YOUR OWN SUCCESS

Several years ago the Reader's Digest carried an article about how each of us carry on a non-vocal conversation with ourselves every minute of the day. At a subconscious level we discuss each aspect of those things that we do throughout the day. This is not the kind of conversation which the crazy man has with himself as he sits alone in the park audibly talking to himself. What this article referred to is that we conduct an intelligent conversation deep within our mind which reacts to those situations and circumstances which we daily face.

This inner narratives which the Bible may be speaking of as "the voice behind our ear" is one which reflects how we feel about external conditions which we face each day. We may react to additional responsibilities thrust upon us by our boss as being unfair. Our inner conversation may reflect the fact that "we already have too much to do now and he still gives me more! What does he think I am—superman?" In another situation our inner voice may react to being stopped by a stoplight as we are driving home from work: "Just what I need—another stoplight to delay me further. Why is it I always get stopped by these stupid lights?"

The conversation may not always be negative in nature. It may reflect a full heart concerning those things which we have been hoping would happen. Perhaps, you have received a long awaited raise in pay. "Finally, they are recognizing me and my talents in this company. If anyone deserves to get this raise, it certainly is me!" This conversation may depict that which you plan to do. "It is almost summertime now, and I am not going to let this vacation time pass without getting the boat I have always wanted! It is sure going to be fun to go fishing on the lake this summer!"

In many cases, this conversation is a reaction to those conditions which affect us. If things go well for us, the conversation is positive. If we face adverse circumstances our narrative will take on the nature of a complaint. A question arises: "Is this the way it is supposed to be?" "Do conditions either good or bad just arise from sources which we are not aware of?" "Or is it possible for us to direct these circumstances according to our desires?" "Can we really determine what it is that we want and then set about to achieve them?"

Let's answer these questions using an illustration. You have just received delivery on a $100,000.00 yacht and you are real excited about it. You are looking forward to getting out on the lake with it and experiencing the freedom of sailing wherever you want to go in it! "Just think of how my friends will also enjoy riding in it and feeling the breeze and the spray of the water as it gently bobs on top of the waves." This is a pleasurable goal which has finally come true for you.

As you board your yacht one morning with plans

that you are going over to the island which is in the middle of the lake and have a pleasant picnic with your friends you realize one specific fact about yachts. You have to pilot them in the right direction in order to reach you intended destination! You are required to correctly guide your yacht so that you can reach your anticipated goal. You begin to think that you cannot just let the yacht go wherever it may drift by itself, because it has to be guided to a predetermined destination. Otherwise disaster could ensue and the ship would be lost. It is no problem for you though, in guiding the yacht, because you have taken instruction in piloting it and you know exactly what to do.

Perhaps you are relating this illustration to the importance of guiding our inner narrative. "Why would it be important to guide this inner conversation we have with ourselves?" "Is it not just random, unimportant thought which come and go according to the whims of the mind?" Consider this verse in Jeremiah 17:10. "I the Lord search the heart and test the inner self to give to everyone according to his ways, in accordance with the fruit of his actions!" The Lord tests the inner self! The Lord considers what thoughts we think about and what we are saying in our inner conversation and then gives to us according to the nature of these thoughts!

It is just like guiding our yacht! We cannot expect to get to the island in the middle of the lake unless we do certain things which are destined to get us there! We have to pilot or steer the yacht directly to the island if we ever expect to have a picnic with our friends on that island. We also have to steer our lives towards certain intended goals we wish to attain. If we let our inner thoughts continue to be of a random, whimsical nature without the influence of direction, how can we ever expect to realize those predetermined goals which we desire? They will not happen by themselves anymore than the yacht will get to the island without specific intelligent direction.

Which is more important? To direct a $100,000.00 yacht to a specific destination, or to direct our lives toward unlimited desires of our hearts? The Lord gives to us according to our ways! What are our ways? Is what we do, in terms of our inner thoughts and narrative, going to result in the achievement of our dreams and desires? Or are we resolved to take pot-luck and only hope that we may get something good out of life? Would you invite your friends to spend the day with you on your boat and then without guidance only hope that it will take you to some nice beach or island upon which you can have a day of rest and recreation? That type of thinking and planning is absurd because it is not goal oriented! Yet, there are people who direct their lives in that most undetermined manner. They hope for something good to happen to them, but feel that if they don't ever get it that "it was just meant to be!"

How to Direct Your Inner Thoughts

We can analyze our inner thoughts to determine their specific nature. If negative, undirected thinking is the nature of your inner narrative, you can immediately change it towards the nature of those things you wish to be evidenced in your life. You can begin to look at each thought, examine it for its value and either emphasize it more strongly if it is what you want to take place in your plan of goals, or if it is of a negative, inflictive nature you may immediately discard it by rejecting that limiting thought. "That thought does not compute!" "I reject that thought!" In this way you can cast it out of your mind and cancel its effect upon you. But you have to constantly direct your inner narrative until it becomes a positive habit which works for you towards those desired goals.

R. Eugene Nichols explained that we can evaluate our inner thinking processes in his book *The Science Of Mental Cybernetics*. He wrote: "We may search the darkroom of our subconscious to discover what we really believe about ourselves. We may evaluate both negative and positive qualities to determine an honest rating of ourself on personality factors, character traits, preferences, attitudes and prejudices."

Ezekiel 8:12 provides an interesting insight into this process. "Son of man, have you seen what the elders of the house of Israel do in the dark, every man in the chambers of his imagery?" We all have our own private thoughts in the imagery chambers of our own mind. Some concede to the whimsical nature of life and take whatever comes to them! Others fight off the negative aspects of the fleeting nature of thoughts and accept only those thoughts which will lead them on to greater personal growth and to reaching those goals they desire. These people are the successful ones because instead of allowing thoughts to dominate them and their potential future success, they take hold of their inner narrative and direct it by introducing those thoughts which they wish to become a reality in their lives. In this manner they can predetermine what they want to occur in their lives and become very successful.

When we carefully consider what we think about in the chambers of our imagination, we predetermine our self-image to insure that it is exactly what we want it to be. If we want to be a success in life, we must think only and always of those successful thoughts which we want to represent us. Then and only then, can the Lord give to us according to the fruit of our actions and according to the doing of our ways. Then we will be successful in our ways and in everything we do we will prosper! (Joshua 1:8).

26

SUCCESS IN BUSINESS

For several years my responsibilities have required me to lecture to various groups of businessmen and salesmen in their companies on the subject of how they could achieve more productivity and realize a greater portion of their potential through being able to more effectively motivate themselves. Essentially, the areas that I explored with them were how to set and accomplish goals by developing an attitude of expectancy with which they could more effectively reach their goals.

When speaking on the subject of motivation I am reminded of the story about two little boys in which the first one explained that he could ask himself a question that he could answer and then get the second boy to ask himself a question that he COULDN'T answer! When his friend agreed to this ridiculous proposition, the first boy asked: "when a rabbit is digging a hole for himself, how can he dig it so that he doesn't leave any dirt around the outside?" The second boy replied: "that's your question, now answer it!" The first boy answered: "he begins digging the hole from the bottom!" The second little boy then asked: "yea, but how does he get to the bottom of the hole first?" The first boy then reminded him that that was his question and that he couldn't answer it!

Through the years many individuals have contributed ideas which were supposed to answer the question as to how you can lead a more motivated life and eventually experience a greater degree of success. Some of these concepts are in direct conflict with each other. Some psychologists believe that motivated behavior begins with motivated thinking while others suggest that it is the result of motivated actions. There are advisors which teach that in order to effectively reach goals you must have a deadline towards which you strive, whereas, other counselors explain that a deadline causes too much stress and inhibits the individual's inner power from giving him a helping hand.

Our plan in this chapter is not to analyze and compare various techniques of setting goals nor of achieving the motivated life, but only to consider them in terms of what the Bible has to say about them.

One of the most important ingredients a person has to work with is a positively motivated attitude! "A positive attitude—that's what you're going to tell us to have!" No, that's not exactly what I am going to talk about although the Bible does mention the importance of having a positive attitude in Proverbs 17:22. "A cheerful heart makes a good cure, but a broken spirit makes the bones dry up!" I Thessalonians 5:16: "Always be cheerful." Proverbs 15:13: "A happy heart makes the face look sunny; but in grief of heart the spirit is broken!" These verses indicate the importance of having a positive attitude in our activities.

Attitude: Our Potential Reflector

Though it is more pleasant to be associated with a person whose outlook is positive rather than negative, I'm talking about the ATTITUDE itself. When I was in school the only thing I ever heard about the subject of attitude was when I had a poor one in my history or science classes. My attitude was fine in mathematics or music or language, but in history they used to tell me that my attitude was poor! I was never sure just what they meant by that term and the teachers never explained how to get rid of the poor attitude, except to study more. I guess the reason for my poor attitude was that I didn't like history or science and therefore didn't study much for those subjects.

Attitude is how you feel towards a certain subject, a specific individual, or a particular job at work. Authorities tell us that one of the most important elements in being productive is that you like what you do. If you dislike your job your attitude will reflect it along with your productivity. Psychologists tell us that it is important to choose a profession that we like because we will be doing it for a long time. While this is true, it doesn't help much if we are presently stuck with something that we don't like and find it is too late to change and already have a lousy attitude.

Have you ever asked yourself: "where do you get your attitude?" "What causes you to have the attitude you now have?" If you have a good one, how did you get it, or if you are not pleased with your present one, how can you change it?

I get many resumes across my desk that have to be analyzed. Because it would be impossible to meet personally with all of the individuals represented, I have to analyze them first on paper. After insuring that they have the qualifications for the job for which they applied, I then try to sense their attitude towards themselves, their former employers and their former responsibilities. Certain guidelines allow me to initially determine what a man thinks about himself and about his potential productivity in our organization. When I have discarded a great number of them which do not fit our needs I then invite several of the potential candidates in for an interview. It is at this time that I listen to this person tell about himself and his abilities and what he thinks he could do for our company. What I am really listening to is his attitude which I can discern from his conversation. Does he or she feel that they can contribute to our company in terms of productivity? Does he wear well with others over a long period of time or do people get tired of him and find it difficult to work with him? Will he be considerate of those on his staff and realize that they are just human when they let him down, or will he be a tyrant in how he manages these people? How will he act with other line officers in meetings and conferences? Will he be tolerant of their ideas or will he want to do things only his way? How is his public relations with suppliers to this company? Will he be able to deal with the public or does he just want to stay in his own office and not have to confront them? It is necessary to know a great many things about a potential executive that we are considering for a position in our company.

All of these items pertain to the man's attitude. If he is to be assigned a sales position it is necessary that he also have an expectant attitude about making sales. He should feel that our product will meet the needs of his potential buyers in such a way that he expects them to purchase it. If he is going to be in a management position and be responsible for others it is necessary that he have an attitude which looks for the potential in those for whom he is responsible. He should be able to point out their strengths and abilities and when discussing their shortcomings do it in such a delicate way as to make them want to overcome them and not become discouraged and defensive about them.

Some personnel officers feel that a man's attitude is the most important element in considering him for a certain responsibility. There are many people who have degrees and specific training in important areas, but if their attitude is bad all the training from the best schools will not make them work effectively with others and positively contribute to a company.

There Goes My Ego

It is my responsibility to work with people in varied fields of endeavor. In addition to sales people, I have to work with teachers, entertainers and recording artists. It is a true fact that most people have an ego problem to one extent or another, but these three categories of people with whom I am in constant contact seem to have the biggest ego problem of all!

Perhaps sales people need a bigger ego to bolster up any feelings of inadequacy that they may experience when confronting a prospect. Perhaps they have chosen the field of selling to prove to themselves that their feelings of inferiority are not true. Or, it might be that they enjoy being the one who is in charge of a conversation as they demonstrate to the prospect the virtues of their product. In any case, their ego is involved in their work and in some cases it can be a big one beating a large bass drum way out in front of them! Why do I know all of this about salesmen's ego? Because I too, have an ego problem! My wife tells me that it isn't as bad as it used to be, but in my moments of truth with myself, I know it is still there and has to be constantly watched! In fact, mine was really big at one time because I was a salesman, teacher and concert artist!

I am not positive that anyone really ever gets over their ego problem but I think they just learn how to handle it so that it doesn't get out of line and turn people off!

We have chosen one particular popular recording and concert artist to represent our organ in concerts around the world. He travels to many cities to perform in concerts and then to explain the many features of the organs to dealers and their staff. Many times Lyn and I work together in these programs. It is totally unfair for one man to have so much talent in his ten fingers, but he has spent many agonizing hours at the keyboard perfecting his enchanting talent and committing to memory a repertoire which seems to be endless. To say that Lyn is a tremendous guy would be to diminish the kind of individual he really is. Lyn has every reason to sport a huge ego and would be completely justified if he did so, but to talk with him in business meetings is to discover that he is just another nice guy. Never does he give an indication that he possesses an international reputation as being one of the greatest theatre organists of all time. He is easy to get along with, is not ruffled if we have to change his schedule around several times even though it takes him and his manager many hours of extra work to readjust other dates he may also have scheduled. Sadly, there are few people like this one with whom to work.

I am not trying to indicate that an ego is all bad, but that it has to be kept in control. An ego can provide a balance between one's sense of self-esteem and any innate feelings of inferiority. The story is told of one psychiatrist who told his patient: "you don't have an inferiority complex; you ARE inferior!" Only when we allow our ego to control our personality and attitude does it become objectionable and interferes with our ability to be productive. A controlled ego can become a motivating partner which adds thrust to the realization of our goals and dreams.

Making An Ego Work For You!

While conducting sales meetings for almost one thousand sales people around the country, I have discovered a simple tactic that makes their ego work for us. It is really an appropriation of another success principle which is found in Proverbs. After I am introduced to each group of salesmen I sometimes sense an attitude on their part which declares: "Why do I have to sit through another sales meeting; I have been selling for ten years now and I don't need another guy from the home office telling me how to get my prospects to sign on the dotted line, particularly when he is no longer on the firing line facing the customers and is stuck in the home office where he doesn't have to deal directly with the public!" I know that this is their attitude because it used to be my own attitude when I had to attend sales meetings over and over again!

I never have claimed to have all of the answers to any particular problems in selling and I don't have all of them now, but I do have a few ideas which have worked for some salesmen and this is the thought with which I usually begin each meeting. There are many really top professional sales people out in the field who could do a better job conducting the meetings than I could ever expect to do and many times they have to sit still and listen to what I have to say. So I try to put things in proper perspective when I talk to them by letting them know that almost any one of them could do a better job of directing this meeting and I should probably sit down and let them run the meeting. "But I am stuck with the job, so let's get it over with together." Many of the people tell me that they received some good ideas from the meeting, but I remind them that I got these ideas from other sales people and just shared the ideas with them. I also remind them that I got a few more ideas while conducting this meeting and will be sharing them with the next group I talk to.

While all of this is a technique with which I prefer to initiate each of the meetings, it happens to be true! For a guy, who was at first scared to death of going into the selling field, to be conducting a meeting for an international company in front of top-notch professionals is the most ridiculous thing I have ever heard of, yet that's my job, and I am trying to learn to do it better each day.

This meeting room technique happens to be supported by the success principle mentioned in Proverbs 11:25: "he who waters, will himself be watered!" Every time I conduct a meeting, I learn something new! I have found that if I make these sales meetings an open-ended meeting, that is, if I let those pros who want to say something which will contribute to the meeting it will do two things: one, it can potentially contribute useful information to others in the meeting, and two, it will allow that salesman's ego to be showcased enough to where his attitude will be receptive to other potential useful ideas presented in the meeting. This method used in sales meetings bears out the effectiveness of this success principle: "he who waters, will himself be watered!"

Many of us find ourselves in various business meetings and conferences in which many personalities and attitudes are intermingling. Each of these people feel that their ideas are the most important and that their solution to the problem is the most effective. When several perspectives conflict with each other, the egos become involved, voices may raise and tempers flare! This will happen each time that anyone is protective only of his own ego and tends to step mercilessly over the egos of his associates. This, of course, is reflective of many things, particularly of a selfish attitude. Again the attitude is the culprit in these situations. The attitude is the outward reflector of the individual's inner concept of his own and others' ego.

Once we learn to protect our associates' ego in our inter-business relationships, we will learn to get others to do almost anything we want them to do. They will not feel that we are trying to attack them and will not be nearly as cautious in dealing with us. In fact, they will usually respond with the same kind of attitude which protects our ego so that we don't have to push it beyond what is good taste.

At one time I was quite involved in writing a special teaching program for the company which required an extensive amount of photography. Chris had a flair for taking pictures even though his major responsibility in our company was in the electronic field. Chris is one of these guys who is talented in many fields and is able to contribute to our company in many ways. I asked him if he would care to assist in this project by offering some advice as to how I could best communicate those ideas I wished expressed through pictures. I explained that photography was not one of my strong points and that I had to rely on someone like himself who was skilled in this field. (He had taught photography in a college at one time.) Since Chris was a willing individual to help in whatever way he could, he suggested that not only was he willing to offer advice but that if I wanted him to actually do the photography for the course of instruction, he would be glad to help.

Of course, I was thrilled that he had offered his help. After the course had been completed, I made certain that our boss knew that it was Chris who had contributed in the area of photography and that it was more professional than many other photographers I had previously used. This statement made in front of Chris to the boss seemed to please him and I noticed in later projects, that any time I wanted Chris's help, he was most willing to assist. I also noticed that he recognized my technique in public relations because in a later project I heard him commenting on the professionalism with which I had done something. This reminds me of what it says in Ecclesiastes 11:1: "Cast your bread upon the waters, for you will find it after many days." Though Chris and I were employing the same technique on each other, it still made working together much easier.

Renewing Our Attitude

We have been considering different kinds of attitudes in this discussion. Suppose you are not completely happy with all aspects of your own attitude and wish to change it in some ways. The Bible suggests that we "renew our mental attitude" in Ephesians 4:23. This is not suggesting that we simply CHANGE our attitude, but that we RENEW it! There's quite a difference between the two! To CHANGE an attitude could be quite difficult, but to RENEW it involves a totally different process!

Suppose that your attitude has been the same for years. You know it but don't know what to do about changing it! Your responsibilities have not changed substantially over the last five to ten years and you have become lax in your approach to your job—not enough to get into difficulty but it is not as vibrant as the first years in which you were involved in your duties. You might say that your attitude has become stagnant because of the lack of renewal through the years. Stagnant water in a pond will begin to stink if it doesn't have the opportunity to change, and an attitude can become stagnant if it is not renewed often!

If you have not changed in some way through the years in what you do you might consider yourself to be in a rut. How can you change your attitude when your job requires that you do it one way and no other way will be accepted? If you really feel that with all of the modern day technology and methodology in production efficiency that you cannot improve upon the way in which you perform your job, then you need to look into your outside interests and use that as a springboard through which to renew your attitude. Do you have a hobby or sport in which you are interested? How about church or club activities to which you can contribute? By giving of yourself, you will receive a renewed attitude which can sustain you in the one way in which you do your job. Some people travel all over the world through the medium of books. I had an uncle who was quite versed in varied subjects relating to many different cultures even though he never left his home town. He had a habit of reading the encyclopedia on one different topic after another. I must admit that that isn't the way I would want to renew my attitude, but at least he had a good attitude towards life!

Goals Can Inspire A Renewed Attitude

Another way in which to renew your attitude is to set some goals for yourself and then make plans to reach them. As we progress through grammar school we have a goal to graduate from one grade into another. Next, we intend to graduate from High School into College. Then comes Graduate School and specialized training. Our goal after Graduate School is to get a nice position with a company which allows us to earn a comfortable income. At that point, many times a person's goal setting stops and so does his progress! It is then that the attitude may begin to deteriorate or become stagnant because of no further personal and business progress. It is possible to become dead-ended in a company because the attitude has not been consistently renewed! Why should our goal setting stop at this point? Why not continue to allow goals and their motivational value to continue to add new perspectives to our attitude and renewed dimension to our life?

The Bible suggests some ideas which may be interpreted to confirm this concept. In Colossians 3:2 it states: "Apply your mind to things above, not to things on earth." Several interpretations are possible in this principle. I wish to direct your thoughts to this possible meaning. Earthly thoughts are those ideas which are all around us; those thoughts which have continually captured our thinking such as, materialism, money, self, sex, our own comfort, our own responsibilities, lack of direction towards higher and more expanded perspectives, etc. Since we become what we think about, if we dwell on these immediate thoughts we will experience little growth towards higher goals.

One of the possible interpretations of this verse could be that if we neglect to immerse ourselves with deeper thoughts and ideas contained in the Bible, we become locked into the same life over and over again. One salesman explained to his boss that he had twenty five years of sales experience. After his boss looked at his sales record and the fact that there was evidence of little growth, he reworded the salesman's statement: "no, you have had one year's experience twenty-five times!"

How can we daily renew our mental attitude? One way is to supply new input to our mental computer. In this verse in Colossians it suggests that we think on those things which are above—higher thoughts—not on things on earth. If we become snagged by old, worn out thoughts which do not contribute to a renewed attitude we will not experience a refreshed attitude and will long for the "good old days" when our present tired out thoughts were fresh and new!

When we program our mind with thoughts of above, these are higher thoughts and are ones which offer us a challenge which will cause our attitude to become fresh, vibrant and exciting! Higher thoughts make us reach out and expand and become a better person than we were yesterday. Business growth is a matter of new ideas constantly being developed; new methods of marketing these ideas which will capture the imagination of the public and cause them to take action in buying a specific product.

Though you may see a specific advertising theme used over and over again in a television commercial, there will be new settings, scripts and characters acting out that theme because people get tired of the same old things thrust at them day after day. We can renew our mental attitude by supplying refreshed and revitalized ideas to our mind. Higher thoughts challenge us to respond with new ways of meeting that challenge! Robert Browning realized this when he wrote: "a man's reach should exceed his grasp!" I have always told my organ students that when setting your goals, to be sure to set them high, because if you don't quite reach them you will be a lot higher than if you had set your goals lower and didn't quite reach them!

I recall certain phases in my life during which the Lord allowed me to respond to the challenge of higher thoughts. When I first realized that God was talking to me when Paul wrote: "I CAN do all things through Christ which strengthens me," I began to take that seriously and to think higher thoughts. After I finished college I went into school teaching. After several years of teaching I realized that though this is a very dedicated profession, I wanted to become involved in something which would reward me directly in a financial way to the extent to which I chose to work. This was one of the reasons I chose sales. The amount of money I would earn was according to how hard I wanted to work and perfect my sales ability. Along the way there were growing pains, of course, but these are natural to the process of becoming a bigger person.

After several years of direct retail selling I realized that again I felt the urge to think higher thoughts. I began to aspire towards becoming a sales manager and trainer of men. I knew that I really would have to think some higher thoughts to be able to respond to this challenge. I studied management books and took several courses in this field. I studied additional sales technique books to provide more resources for my mind to work with and finally made it to the position of sales manager of a company.

The next challenge was to become Vice President and General Manager of a string of music stores. After thinking the necessary appropriate higher thoughts and doing the work necessary to justify this responsibility, I achieved this goal. This position afforded a great challenge to my abilities but also provided great satisfaction to see sales rise as a result, in part, of my efforts.

Next came an even higher challenge to which I responded. This was to be Sales Promotion Manager of an international company. At that time this was the big goal and a position sought by many. It was only after thinking those thoughts which are above which included Paul's "I CAN" principle, that I was able to attain this plum of a goal.

As I reflect upon these steps in my own personal growth, I would have made only one change in the original plan. I would have reached out for these challenges sooner than I did. I would have appropriated God's power to reach higher goals as quickly as I felt I could. Emerson said: "Do the thing and you shall have the power."

I carry in my wallet this verse:

> "Bite off more than you can chew
>   Then chew it.
> Plan for more than you can do,
>   Then do it.
> Point your arrow at a star,
>   Take good aim and there you are.

Arrange more time than you can spare,
　　Then spare it.
Take on more than you can bear,
　　Then bear it.
Plan your castle in the air.
　　Then, with God's help, you are there!"

In essence, this is the combined meaning of these two success principles: "to renew your mental attitude" by "thinking on higher thoughts!"

You might react to my goal setting plan with "that's nice that you have been able to expand your goals in reaching a higher plateau each time! You must be happy that you have finally reached a level in which you can be content!" Perhaps that is true, but in each of the levels of progress I found myself to be content—not in the sense that I wanted to remain at each of the levels, but that I was able to attain these degrees of advancement through applying the "I CAN" success principle. Once again the contentment realized in my present position is only in what I have been able to achieve through God's power and now I am ready for the next step. I have now just gotten to the point that I can clearly see what's really out there waiting for me to be challenged. Now I have some goals set which are really going to be fun to reach out for! I have the next one clearly visualized as I did with each of the other steps. In fact, it activates my panic button to not have a goal clearly visualized because of the success principle which says: "without a vision (a clearly visualized goal) the people run wild!" I've already wasted enough time, I can't afford to lose any more time by running wild without a goal!

The more progressive companies are strong on goal setting. Management ask department heads to specify on paper what they expect their departments to accomplish in a given time period. Department heads discuss with individuals what they expect to be able to do to contribute to the company's growth.

Most companies expect at least a ten percent growth each year. Without this moderate progress, signs of stagnancy may appear. A company can't grow unless the employees cause it to grow by increasing their personal productivity. An employee does this by improving the way he does his job and by growing as an individual. Finally, personal growth is the result of meeting the challenges of setting higher, more stimulating goals.

Setting Individual Goals

Just how does an individual set goals? Paul says that a runner in a race runs to win; a boxer fights to win not as "punching the air." Goals cannot be so far out of realistic reach that they are just words or they may not motivate us to appropriate action. They have to be set within our conceptual powers; within the bounds of our believability, or they won't put the needed thrust into our plans which make it possible to reach them!

Paul said: "this one thing I do" in relationship to his goals. Our dedication towards our goals should reflect a singleness of purpose, a straightforward approach which will lead us to what we want. James 1:7 says that a double-minded man should not expect to receive anything from the Lord.

The first step in setting a goal is to determine what is the first major step we wish to accomplish. An unfocused camera produces a blurred, undecipherable picture. The picture of our goals has to be decisive, determined, and clearly defined. It has to be understood in terms of "this one thing I do!"

I have used many methods through which to clarify my one major objective such as writing them down on paper to enable me to see them in a more total perspective. Forming them into affirmations and then repeating them many times each day also helps to identify them more clearly in my mind.

When your goals are clearly represented in your mind you will find an inner power surge which will add thrust to the attainment of your goals.

Once you have determined exactly what it is you want to achieve, then set a date upon which you intend to reach it. Review this statement as often as you can, even several times daily. If you don't make your goal by the first date, change it to another date later on. After all, you set the date so you can change it if necessary. If you find that you have to change that date too many times, maybe the goal is set too high or you aren't willing to do those things necessary to reach the goal.

It must be quite obvious that after setting a goal and a deadline you can't just sit back and expect it to happen without any sacrifice or work on your part. Analyze the goal and decide what is the first thing that you can do to help reach it. Sometimes it is helpful to break that goal down into smaller parts and set dates for each step. By reaching a larger goal one step at a time it becomes easier to visualize and to attain.

Personal Growth Chart

A personal growth chart is quite a helpful method of encouraging personal growth. When I did this on one side of a piece of paper I listed the major strengths I felt I had under the title "Strengths." On the other side under "Weaknesses" I listed those areas in which I felt I needed personal growth! After I had finished doing this work I found a way through which I was able to experience a great deal of personal growth and incidentally, dramatically increase my income. Here is what my personal growth chart looked like:

Strengths	Weaknesses
1. Have a strong drive to achieve.	1. Too curt with people.
2. I am willing to work hard.	2. Impatient.
3. Like to sell people on ideas.	3. Not careful enough in my work.
4. I am creative and have lots of new ideas.	4. Not enough long range planning.
5. I am good at writing copy.	5. Lack self-confidence.
6. I have good health.	
7. I have a positive attitude.	

Once I determined my strengths, I counted them up; a total of 7 strong points. Then I divided them into my income and determined (according to this way of calculating) that each one contributed a specific amount to my income. Then I looked at the weaknesses and added them up: a total of 5. I figured that if I could overcome them one at a time that, theoretically, they should add the same amount that the strengths did to my income.

With that in mind, I set out to overcome each one of the weaknesses. I found that it was a good theory, but didn't work the way I thought it would! Instead, it worked better than what I had planned! As I finally overcame each weakness my income had gone up a greater extent than what I had originally thought it would. It turned out to be well worth the effort involved!

The Bible seems to indicate that personal growth is necessary for progress towards success. III John 2 says, "Beloved, my wish for you above all things is that you prosper, even as your soul prospers!" A temptation in goal setting is to wish for things themselves and not for personal growth, yet in this verse it is possible that the phrase "even as your soul prospers" indicates the need for personal growth as a necessary accompaniment to the motivational power of desiring things. While the thrust received from acquiring "things" is energizing in its ability to make us reach out for goals, our motivational sails need to be set for becoming a stronger and more dynamic individual. "To BE is to HAVE" might be a paraphrased version of this verse!

As we experience personal growth through goal setting we will experience the thrill of accomplishment. The inspiration achieved from expanding our sphere of activity will provide an excitement which will motivate us towards setting even higher goals.

One of the areas of growth we will recognize is the kind of enthusiastic attitude we will begin to have! Let's look at some of the characteristics of an enthusiastic attitude!

Aptitude or Attitude?

"An individual's attitude is more important than his aptitude" was the statement made by a successful salesmanager. He had been with the newspaper firm for over forty years! Through an enthusiastic attitude, a growing individual can positively present his abilities and multiply the effectiveness of his aptitude. However, a dimly lit display of one's attitude covers his aptitudes with a dinginess which often appears as a lack of self-confidence.

The Bible speaks of being enthusiastic in your activities: "whatever your hand finds to do, do it with all your might!" If a job is worthy of any effort at all, do it enthusiastically! My two sons and I once built a bedroom in the attic of our home. Some of the framing didn't work out exactly as it should have been. One of my sons said: "it'll be alright, dad, since we'll be covering it over with wallboard anyway!" While it was true that we could have hid our mistakes with wallboard, I wanted to teach them something about "what your hand finds to do!" I explained to them that "if you haven't got the time to do it correct the first time, how are you going to find the time to do it over again?" We all felt better about the kind of job we did after we ripped out some of the structure and did it again—correctly!

The Bible challenges us to be "filled with the Spirit!" It also explains that the Spirit is the energizer within us. If we are filled with the Spirit we are energetic and enthused. The Greek word "entheos" means "in God" or "God in you," or filled and energized with the Spirit. I sincerely question those downhearted and dejected Christians as to whether they are truly filled with the Spirit!

Being enthusiastic generates its own energy. The more enthusiastic you are in your activities the more energy you will have to approach them, and the more energy you have the more enthusiastic you will become! It is a positive power cycle which is exciting and powerful to be involved in.

I had just finished dinner in a coffee shop and had been watching the waitresses as they performed their duties. There were four or five of them all busily taking care of their stations with a bounce and a positive flair which didn't happen naturally. I knew that there must be a reason for this display of positive enthusiasm and I soon found out why!

The manager of the coffee shop made an appearance for a short time and I watched him as he also went about his duties with a happy attitude radiating from his face. I checked the day of the week—no, it wasn't payday, nor the day before a holiday. Each person's attitude generated enthusiasm among each other, and then added to the customer's pleasure of eating there! I could easily determine why this restaurant was so crowded with customers!

After watching the crew for a while, I figured that this positive attitude was in evidence because the manager took time to make sure that everyone was happy with what they were doing and that there were no potential problems developing. I watched as the manager spoke to each girl for just a moment and inquired if there was anything he could do to help. This concern and interest on his part for their particular situations showed them that they were important to him and that he wanted to make sure that everything was okay with them!

Unfortunately, the reverse is also true. While enthusiasm is contagious, so is an attitude of dejection. A moment or two inquiring about our associate's problems can keep the inter office relationship on a positive note and maintain the spirit of enthusiasm among a staff. But, put one clinker with a negative attitude in a staff and soon it's like the one bad apple in a barrel.

An enthusiastic attitude becomes a habit which affects all of those people around you. The Bible says "provoke one another unto love and good works" (KJV). The Berkeley Version uses the word "stimulate" instead of "provoke!" A positive, enthusiastic attitude is a stimulating and provoking attitude (not negatively, but inspirationally) which attracts others to itself. The Bible says that we should "let our light shine." Light eliminates the darkness—it's not the other way around—just as an enthusiastic person can turn around a group of negative people to good works. What a challenge we have from God's Word to be that person in our office or home!

Proverbs records that "all the days of the poor are unfortunate, but the glad-hearted has a continual feast." Little thought is required as to which is the most desirable of these two situations. And management doesn't take much time to decide upon which kind of person is given the next promotion to a position of higher responsibility.

Arthur Taylor, the forty-one year old President of CBS, was quoted as saying: "It is unnecessary for a man to use deceit, cheating and lying as his method of getting ahead in business!" It was his suggestion that an individual who actively pursues personal growth through employing proven success principles will ultimately triumph in his career. Taylor is a living testimony of this fact!

Though the success principles presented in this book only partially uncover the many exciting concepts found in the Bible, they do represent many of the most important ingredients to living a successful life as presented by the many success authors quoted in this book. The thrill of personalizing these success principles is found in the fact that the Bible contains a guarantee—not just a promise—that we will be successful if we daily apply and live these principles (Joshua 1:8).

27

HOW TO APPLY
THE SUCCESS PRINCIPLES

Perhaps at this point, a lot of concepts are whirling around in your head. As you have read these success principles and the fact that they have been first presented to us in the pages of the Holy Bible, you have recognized that they are not new ideas as some of the recent success authors have led you to believe. They are tried and true concepts of success which have been with us for literally hundreds of years.

As I have presented these ideas in various meetings in different parts of the country, individuals have asked me "how can I get all of these principles working for me right away?" Now that they have been introduced to these success principles, they recognize that they are void in their life in those areas. They seemed to be surging with a desire to initiate the potential of these principles as quickly as possible.

I wish I could have handed them this book and explained that they should engage in an all out pursuit of the message of these pages. Instead, I had to challenge them to discover the material in the way in which I had to find it—through much study and meditation upon the principles contained in the Word of God.

However, if I had this book at that time I would have suggested that they engage in the following plan of attack in order to get these principles working for them as fast as possible.

A Successful Plan of Attack

Charles M. Schwab, President of the United States Steel Corporation, encouraged his management staff to use a technique each morning which would assist them in organizing their responsibilities in a way that would result in getting the most accomplished for the energy exerted. It is a simple technique and one that I can personally testify as to its effectiveness.

Mr. Schwab would suggest that each morning before they started any of their responsibilities that they form a list of those jobs which had to get done that day. He would suggest that they list each of the responsibilities as they came to mind and when they were all represented on the list, then assign a priority number to each one. They were to pick the one which was the most important and assign priority number one to it, etc., until each item had been given a number of relative importance.

The executive would then methodically begin to discharge his duties according to a predetermined, logical plan which would provide him with an organized approach to his responsibilities. Charles Schwab found that his staff could produce greater results following this plan not because they worked harder, but because they worked smarter!

As you consider the application of these success principles to your life, consider Mr. Schwab's plan of attack. Only you know which principles need attention first, and which ones come next; however, the important thing is to approach them in an organized fashion.

The principles themselves will actually tell you how to apply them to your life. The simple basic truth which declares: "as a man thinks, so is he" challenges us to consider what we think about at all times. As we make our priority list of success principles and review it each morning, we will be carefully considering what we think about. Just as Mr. Schwab found that his men worked better when organized, we think better when organized.

The "G-I-G-O" principle (Good In, Good Out—Garbage In, Garbage Out) tells us that if we want the evidence of success in our activities, we should dwell upon the kind of input which will bring forth success. Various guiding principles direct us along the way such as "above all that you watch, guard over your heart [subconscious mind] for out of it come the sources of life!" Also, "be careful to what you listen!" Another directive principle: "Bring into captivity every mental perception!" "Think on those things which are above, and not on things of the earth." "Daily renew your mental attitude."

The essential message of these verses is that we will get back what we put in. If we plant radishes, we will get radishes—AFTER THEIR KIND! If a cook decides that while he is assembling all of the ingredients for a cake that he will think one little negative thought and put just a bit of poison into that cake, you know the results. This can be the result of one little negative thought when we approach God with our plans. If we doubt at all, when we ask God for something, it becomes a personal affront to God. In essence, we insult God when we ask Him for something with doubt in our hearts. This is why faith is so important in all of our activities. The "I CAN" principle of Paul which evidences the "Expectancy of Success" in all of our endeavors is the balance point upon which the attainment of our desires hinge. "Everything is possible for a believer!"

When I first began to consider all of the many principles of success which seemed to be vital to the attainment of my desires, I found that it was literally beyond my abilities to accomplish! We hear much about how necessary it is to ask God to help us in our lives, but I don't recall hearing much about how He actually does help us! I had a real dilemma! I asked God to help me, but I didn't have enough faith to believe that He really would help me! God is original in the way in which He works with each of us, and all I can report is what the Bible told me to do, and how He worked with me! I believe that these ideas will work for you too!

Receiving is dependent upon believing, but, I didn't have enough faith to believe, so I didn't receive! However, the Word of God shows us a way out of this maze! The more I tried to apply these principles the more discouraged I became until I began to realize that you cannot FORCE success, you have to LET it happen for you! Now what does this mean? Robert Townsend concurs in this concept in his book, *Up the Organization!* He writes: "anything which is directly sought, is rarely ever attained! It is the by-product of some worthwhile effort or cause!" If success is sought for the sake of success—that of showing off to the Jones, it will be difficult to find!

The Scriptures also support this concept: "you covet and you do not possess ... because you ask amiss!" This statement seems only to complicate the attainment of success even more by suggesting that not only do you have to apply the principles correctly, but now your motives have to be correct as you do it! Another principle, however, will clear up this situation. "Seek first the Kingdom of God, and ALL these things will be added unto you!" If we seek success for success sake, we probably will miss the mark; however, if we seek first the Kingdom of God (which just happens to include the success principles) we will receive success as a by-product.

As we seek the Kingdom of God, we are trying to model ourselves after Christ. We are doing what the Scripture says: "to be built up as living stones into a spiritual house!" As we pattern ourselves after Christ by applying the success principles he taught, we will receive prosperity as a by-product of our efforts. The Psalms speak of this kind of person in Chapter One.

> "His delight is in the law of the Lord,
>   and His law he ponders day and night.
> He is like a tree planted by streams of water,
>   that yields its fruit in its season,
> whose leaf does not wither;
>   and everything he does shall prosper."

About this time in my experience, I realized that I wanted to apply these principles to my life as quickly as possible, not for the sake of success, but because I truly believed that the kind of life which would result would be the most peaceful, even though the world exhibited deferred-payment-tension and atomic-age-troubles. It also became most exciting as I saw these principles evidencing themselves in my life as I was being built up in the faith (the Lord only knew how desperately I needed to grow in grace ... well, maybe my wife knew, too). Of course, down deep I wasn't going to object to the success which was going to be a by-product of these efforts.

How To Make Success a Habit

What I needed to know was how to quickly appropriate these success principles in my life. I have discovered that when I have a question this important, that if I present it to God through prayerful meditation, eventually the answer will present itself—and what an answer it usually is! I asked God how to accomplish this task of getting these success principles working in a positive manner for me. Sometimes God doesn't answer a question with simple directions which we may find on the back of an instant cake mix: "mix together in a bowl, add one egg, two cups of milk, and place in the oven for 25 minutes!" He will expose you to various concepts, ideas and principles which when all mixed together form a powerful answer to your question. He allowed me to consider some ideas which I had first been exposed to when I was studying the piano. When I was learning to play the piano, one of the important principles of correct practice is that it takes many repetitions to learn to play something. When I learned to play "Kitten on the Keys" I had to go over and over certain tricky fingering patterns hundreds of times until I could instinctively react with the correct finger responses. It is no exaggeration to report that each line of the song required thousands of slow repetitions of practice before the delegation of the correct fingering requirements could be turned over to the subconscious mind. Literally, I had to make a habit of playing that song correctly!

Perhaps you recall how much practice was required when you learned to type. After you initially learned where each letter of the alphabet was on the typewriter keyboard, it took just plain old repetitive practice to gain speed when typing. How many times did you fall off the bicycle before you eventually demonstrated your ability to balance the two wheeled vehicle? Again, the power of repetition in learning was in evidence!

The same principle is necessary in learning to appropriate the success principles! When we read a book or listen to a lecturer present ideas, we forget 40% of the ideas after 20 minutes; 90% after one week and retain only 5% of the content after two weeks. Why? Because it is nearly impossible to be exposed to these ideas more than once under these circumstances. Unless we read a book more than once we will not gain the advantage of repetition in learning. The problem is, of course, how many times have we read a book more than once? Madison Avenue Advertising Agencies realize the potency of repetitive advertising. Think back about how many times you have seen any one television commercial. I am sure that you have long ago lost count. An example of the power of repetition in advertising lies in this question: "What is Crest?" The most predictable answer is that it is a toothpaste! Why? Because the repetition of the television commercials have changed our thinking from the other meanings, which may have been "the top of a hill," or "the crest of the moon." Repetition, indeed, is powerful in its ability to form a habit response within us! Studies have shown that four year old children know how to hold a guitar properly before they even know the name of the musical instrument. Why? Because, according to these tests, they have seen others playing a guitar so many times on television. Again, repetition has caused appropriate action!

Repetitive exposure to an idea as being necessary for resultant determined action is not a new concept with any of the recent success writers, because it was first presented in the Bible many years ago.

Peter realized this problem back in ancient Rome around 68 A.D. In II Peter 1:10, he explained that "if you PRACTICE these things (success principles) you will never stumble." In verse twelve he writes again: "I will take care always to REMIND you of these matters." (Second exposure.) Then, again he states in verse fifteen: "I will make every effort to enable each one of you to keep these things IN MIND after I am gone!"

He sensed the importance of repetitive exposure to the principles in the Bible to such an extent that he even made sure that someone continued presenting the ideas to the early followers after he was gone.

When I first read this passage in II Peter 1, I immediately realized that this was my answer! I had been insisting that my organ and piano students practice repetitively to effectively learn the necessary fingering patterns, so why shouldn't I approach the success principles in the same manner! Why not literally make a habit of the success principles? Now how do you practice a success principle? It is NOT like a fingering pattern that you can rehearse repetitively on a keyboard, nor is it like trying to learn to ride a bicycle! So how does one approach learning a success principle in a repetitive fashion so that it becomes a habit? Again, I went to prayer about this matter.

The answer had been there all along in another success principle, but I was just now ready to understand how to appropriate it. Remember my original dilemma? I needed more faith to believe that what I asked God for that I would receive. If I had more faith....! Then the full impact of the next success principle hit my understanding! "Faith comes by hearing!" There it was, just as simple as that—faith comes by hearing! Well, why didn't I have more faith already? Hadn't I been hearing faithful ministers of the Word of God all of my life in churches and Bible studies? Then the Lord focused my attention on the principle of repetition and applied it to the new principle, and here was the complete answer! "Faith comes by REPETITIVELY hearing the Word of God!" I had been approaching the acquisition of faith in an unorganized manner. What I needed was the Charles Schwab approach to the responsibility of getting more faith. I needed to list those success principles I wanted to acquire in the order of importance as the Holy Spirit led me in this matter!

Next, I needed to hear them repetitively until success really became a habit! Could I get my pastor to preach the same sermon over and over again until I felt I knew the principles enough to be ready for the next one? That didn't seem to be practical! The way that I was finally able to absorb these concepts was to record various verses on cassette tape which dealt with each of the success principles discussed in this book. I would ask the Lord to lead me to the verses which He felt were important for me to hear on a repetitive basis. I would read them myself on the tape because only I was going to hear them, and if I made a mistake or two I could overlook that.

Incidentally, there is something quite motivational about hearing yourself on a recording. When you couple that concept with the eternal Words of God expressed in each of these success principles, you have something really powerful going for you!

Not only did I record each principle on cassette tape, but I would include various comments that would be directed to point my thinking towards the correct appropriation of the power of these principles. I found that the Holy Spirit helped me with these comments. They were, in some cases, positive comments that I had heard a preacher talk about, or they might have been positive affirmations which challenged me to reach out for more of what the Lord offered me. I would also record various favorite chapters or even books of the Bible which I particularly enjoyed hearing on other cassette tapes. Chapters like the love chapter, or some of the writings of Paul the Apostle.

The book of Proverbs, I believe, is a most practical guidebook for the modern businessman. In its pages are found hundreds of solid business principles which are relevant to the day in which we live. I have recorded the first ten chapters on one thirty minute cassette tape, chapters 11 through 20 on a second one, and the remaining eleven chapters on a third tape. As of this writing, I have listened to the entire book of Proverbs at least 150 times! Still I find new gems of wisdom each time I listen to it.

The beauty of approaching the appropriation of the success principles in this manner, is that you don't FORCE these principles upon you, you merely let them have their effect upon you! It is like the Proverbs say: "roll your work upon the Lord and your plans will be achieved!" Or another Proverb: "it is the blessing of the Lord which brings riches, and toiling will add nothing to it!" Let the Lord fulfill His guarantee to you of success and prosperity! But you have to do your part, which is to be built up in the faith by hearing (repetitively) the Word of God. Then you will have His complete guarantee going for you: "my Word will not return unto Me void!"

It will be my continuing prayer for each of you as you read the Greatest Success Book of All Time—The Bible—that you will discover as I have that it alone is the most dynamic and exciting book one can ever read!

> "Constantly remind the people about these laws, and you yourself must think about them every day and every night so that you will be sure to obey all of them. For only then will you succeed."
>
> Joshua 1:8 (TLB)